CAPABILITY
BROWN

And His Landscape Gardens

CAPABILITY BROWN

And His Landscape Gardens

Sarah Rutherford

FSC
www.fsc.org

MIX
Paper from
responsible sources
FSC® C023419

Published in 2016 by
National Trust Books
1 Gower Street
London WC1E 6HD

An imprint of Pavilion Books Company Ltd

ISBN: 9781909881549

A CIP catalogue record for this book is available from the
British Library.

20 19 18 17 16
10 9 8 7 6 5 4

Reproduction by Colourdepth, UK
Printed and bound in Italy by Lego S.p.A.

This book can be ordered direct from the publisher
at the website: www.pavilionbooks.com, or try your
local bookshop. Also available at National Trust shops and
nationaltrustbooks.co.uk

Historic England is a government service championing
England's heritage and giving expert, constructive advice.

PREVIOUS PAGE | Lancelot 'Capability' Brown (1716–83), the
Shakespeare of the art of gardening (Richard Cosway, c.1770–75).

LEFT | Brizlee Tower by Robert Adam, the spectacular focus at
Hulne Park, Alnwick, Northumberland.

RIGHT | At Audley End, Brown's simple palette is used to great
effect in a naturalistic way using water, grass and trees (William
Tomkins, 1788).

Contents

Introduction

Why 'Capability' Brown?

The omnipotent magician, monarch of landscape, a very able master, a man of wit, learning and great integrity; this unique and lavish praise was heaped upon Lancelot 'Capability' Brown in his lifetime for his genius in transforming unpromising countryside into beautiful parks that seemed to be only the work of Dame Nature. He epitomised the emerging cult of the countryside, of the landscape tamed by man and made artistically productive.

One of the most remarkable men in an age of pioneering talent, he was engaging, capable, humorous and hugely productive, but shunned the limelight. His extraordinary client list included the king, six prime ministers and half the House of Lords. Although his fame may now have dimmed, his masterpieces speak for him, many of which we still enjoy today. The 300th anniversary of his birth in 2016 has been the catalyst to rediscover him and his artistry, and reinstate him at the heart of the Pantheon of British genius. This is the opportunity to tell his triumphant story and to discover what this Northumbrian of yeoman stock was trying to do and just why he was so successful.

BELOW | Blenheim Palace, Oxfordshire, the epitome of Brown's genius. This painting hangs in Winston Churchill's study at Chartwell (English School, 1770s).

Brown: the Shakespeare of gardening

'Capability' Brown is the most talented and prolific of the artists who created the thousands of English Landscape Gardens – gardens on a large scale that seem natural and irregular. This is a great accolade considering that the English Landscape Garden is arguably the greatest contribution Britain has made to the visual arts worldwide. Brown's artistry often goes unnoticed as it blends so subtly into the landscape and its impact has been mostly overlooked. He is associated with more than 250 sites covering 200 square miles in total.

With Brown as its chief exponent, the influence of the English Landscape Garden became ubiquitous, stretching out over Europe to Russia, India, the United States and beyond. As Horace Walpole, Georgian writer, arbiter of taste and son of the first prime minister, put it, 'We have given the true model of gardening to the world. Let other countries mimic our taste.' Brown was our ambassador extraordinaire, even though he never left Britain. In a nutshell, his fame rests on the simplicity of his artistic formula and its innate appeal, the enormous number of commissions he undertook and his memorable nickname.

What's in a name? A name is vital in business, offering a snappy image and strong corporate identity to dominate the market. Lancelot Brown is an unusual name, but his famous nickname 'Capability' Brown denotes someone extraordinary who changed the face of Britain forever. His soubriquet 'Capability' came from his habit of advising prospective clients that their grounds had 'great capabilities' – in today's parlance 'potential'. It is said that he obtained this nickname early on in his career at Croome: 'from the answer he made to Lord Coventry; when, having been shewn the place to which much had been done before, his Lordship asked him how he liked it? *Why, my Lord, the place has its capabilities*' (*Morning Post*, 30 July 1774).

ABOVE | Brown was both design genius and businessman. Prime Minister Pitt the Elder urged him, 'Go you and adorn England', to which Brown replied 'Go you and preserve it' (After Sir Nathaniel Dance-Holland, c.1775).

Brown's quirky name is familiar to people with an interest in history, but few know what he actually did. We still admire his works and genius in the English Landscape Garden, albeit often unwittingly. He did not invent his style, but he was enormously successful in his day as a visionary landscape designer. The radical thing about his landscape gardens was to sweep away the formal garden rooms, straight canals, pools and avenues, and set out instead smooth, sinuous lines, open sweeps of parkland and swooping lines of lakes and rivers. All was revealed in one majestic panorama, unfolded one view at a time as the visitor passed through it.

Like the rooms we expect to find in a house, the landscape garden has standard areas. It contains a park, garden and pleasure ground, drives, kitchen garden and often, and most prized, a great sinuous artificial river or sheet of water, all enclosed by woodland belts, with the country house at its heart. As a craftsman as well as an artist Brown knew how to take the raw materials and natural features of bedrock and fuse these elements into a framework unique to each place, overlaid and ornamented with myriad plants. Having done so, he left his artistry in many of the 250 and more places he is connected with, most obviously clumps of trees framing views and river-like lakes. Many other landscapers followed this formula too but his was a rare ability to see the design that would embrace the whole scale of a great landscape.

Brown's visionary capabilities, with 'a poet's feeling and a painter's eye', far outlived his age and still affect and influence us today. The poetry of his artistry is still expressed in the landscapes he created, but often we need to look hard to tease out his mastery. He was as influential in his visual and physical effects on the British landscape as those other great British achievers, Thomas Telford, James Brindley and Isambard Kingdom Brunel, who built roads, canals, bridges and railways of great robustness and longevity that shouted their origins in human endeavour. In contrast, Brown's works were so subtle and naturalistic that they are often entirely missed for what they are. For at a glance they appear to be entirely natural rather than massive works of art, combining artistry, horticulture and engineering.

We cannot miss Telford's road through North Wales, to Holyhead. Brindley gave shape to the English canal network that still meanders across the country and Brunel's railways and Clifton Suspension Bridge in Bristol dominate their surroundings. While these are very evident triumphs of man's ingenuity, Brown's mastery does not shout loudly. Instead he was

the master of subtlety, making the most of what was there already. So much so, in fact, that by his death in 1783, after 40 years of non-stop park-making, it was said that, 'Such … was the effect of his genius that when he was the happiest man, he will be least remembered; so closely did he copy nature that his works will be mistaken'. Ironically the rather self-important architect William Chambers, one of Brown's disgruntled competitors, turned this into a complaint that Brown's grounds 'differ very little from common fields, so closely is nature copied in most of them'. Chambers with his architect's ego had missed the subtle point.

ABOVE | This view from the Long Gallery, Croome, Worcestershire, sums up Brown's 'capabilities': in the house he built, overlooking one of his greatest parks, to his iconic Cedar of Lebanon.

CHAPTER 1

Brown, his world and his life

Brown's recipe for success

So why was Lancelot Brown dubbed the Omnipotent Magician? A unique set of circumstances presented themselves and Brown was quite simply the right man, in the right place, at the right time. He took the opportunies offered and England became a more beautiful place as a result.

The world recognises the Landscape Garden as one of England's greatest contributions to the visual arts. Brown was certainly the most prolific of these artists, probably the most talented, and his works survive all over England and into Wales. He swept away formality in the garden, using wavy lines and flinging open the view across the ha-ha into the park. His prolific inspiration revolutionised the English garden style we still admire. His work even had a spiritual dimension and continues to refresh the weary urban dwellers who crowd into the likes of Blenheim Palace and Croome during their precious hours of recreation.

Professionally, like many other landscapers, he understood the form of the raw site with the eye of a land surveyor. His unique talent combined his artistic and engineering eye. He quickly took in the capabilities of the raw agricultural land for conversion to a living work of art, and homed in on its ornamental potential. He balanced the essential parts of a landscape park, depending on its unique qualities. Also an architect, he could produce an elegant house, stables or any type of engaging garden building in styles of the time, particularly the classical and Gothic, as the client preferred, and many of his own buildings populate his parks. This was all combined with his innate business sense, quick working and unshakeable honesty.

Having daringly abandoned his origins as an estate steward's son in remote Northumberland, Brown became the public face of the English landscape movement. He was addicted to hard work, with thousands of miles spent on horseback crisscrossing England between clients and their estates, despite bouts of ill health. None of his contemporaries were so prolific over such an outstanding period in landscape design, just when the English landscape garden peaked in popularity (although Brown was helped by a team of assistants in his office and out on the ground). Add to this his personality: as Walpole said, he was endowed with 'wit, learning and great integrity'. He was engaging and humorous, entertaining and warm, and knew his place with his clients, but was not overly subservient. Most importantly, he not only knew his job, but also how to deal with self-opinionated and powerful clients, a useful trait for anyone in business.

PREVIOUS PAGE | Stowe, Buckinghamshire, where Brown first made his name in the 1740s. His emerald green sweeping lawn replaced a fussy parterre, his prototype for Blenheim.

He had unique access to the ear and purse of the whole spectrum of the ruling classes. His client list, including royalty and many of the wealthiest and most influential men in the kingdom, has probably never been equalled by anyone else. Nor did his rivals have Brown's reputation as such a congenial man, easy to employ and good company for his employers, many of whom looked forward to his visits.

Indeed, Lancelot dropped dead after a night out at dinner with his greatest patron, the 6th Earl of Coventry. The Earl was a friend of long standing who had commissioned Brown's early master work, Croome, Worcestershire, some 30 years before, and kept calling him back to develop it still further. Lord Coventry was one of those visionary 'Earls of Creation' and other nobles who developed their estates under the influence of classical philosophies and the Grand Tour of Italy. He warmly paid tribute to Brown's ingenuity, his inimitable and creative genius, for as the Earl generously said, 'Croome … was entirely his creation, and, I believe, originally as hopeless a spot as any in the island', fashioning a master work out of a 'morass'.

Though of relatively humble origins, Brown had a following of the richest and most powerful men in England, a select group of whom banded together not once but twice to petition his cause to be made Royal Gardener, successfully second time around. Two of his employers, Lord Coventry at Croome and the redoubtable Jemima Grey at Wrest Park, Bedfordshire, put up elegant garden monuments attesting to the skill of his works and the congeniality of his personality. Amazingly, none of this turned his head. He did not aspire to power, political influence or unearned riches, but remained the same hard-working genius of the English Landscape Garden.

The circumstances of the age allowed Brown to crystallise the landscape movement as he surfed the wave from formal to informal gardens, assisted by burgeoning national wealth, peace at home in Britain and improving transport links. In his landscapes Brown was expressing his artistic abilities, creating scenic and plastic works of genius, altering the fabric of the country in what became an iconic English style. Few of us realise this as we survey the pastoral delights of great estates such as Croome, Wimpole or Blenheim, because the style is now so deeply embedded in our national character. Artists and poets were representing only second-hand the scenes they admired. Brown actually provided the inspiration for some of these other artists' work that can still be admired today. Turner, for example, painted many of Brown's scenes at Petworth that can still be compared with the reality outside the windows.

Brown was one of a group of outstanding designers who served the wealthiest Georgians with great success. Other star names of the period ring in our ears and still affect our taste today and inevitably their paths crossed Brown's.

Thomas Chippendale (1718–79) is the only furniture maker most people have ever heard of. This Yorkshireman forged a niche as 'the carpenter to the quality', and still his graceful styles are sought after and enjoyed. His and Brown's lives have parallels of contemporary artistic genius and eminence among an especially talented generation. Chippendale too was recognised as a star in his particular firmament, being named the Shakespeare of English furniture makers. Both ran similar artisan craftsmen businesses based on personal services to their wealthy clients. Chippendale's business blossomed early on, and by 1755 he employed some 40–50 artisans to make the furniture he designed, cultivating clients and promoting the business in a similar business model to Brown's.

Perhaps the greatest difference was Chippendale's master stroke that immortalized him early in his career: he published his designs in a hugely popular pattern book *The Gentleman and Cabinet-Maker's Director* (1754). This brilliant self-promotion stimulated commissions and spread his designs throughout Britain, Europe and the Colonies in a way that Brown never attempted, nor needed to. Chippendale had more than 70 major clients (to Brown's 250 and more), including many of Brown's starriest patrons, and 600 pieces of furniture are attributed to him.

Chippendale worked in similar enormous sums to Brown. Sometimes the two worked on the same places, alongside other creative stars. Chippendale's most valuable and extensive commission (and one of the most expensive of the time anywhere), furnished Harewood House near Leeds, begun for Edwin Lascelles in 1767 and costing some £10,000. Lascelles spent a mere £7,000 with Brown, who, even so, produced a park that is one of his finest. Despite his great success and recognition, Chippendale suffered financial problems. At his death his household furnishings were worth only £28, unlike Brown who managed his affairs on a more even keel and left at least £10,000 behind him. Chippendale doesn't sound as likeable as Brown, with a sense of his own superiority, and was definitely treated as a tradesman by his clients, unlike Brown who occupied a unique hybrid position with his clients, and architects such as Robert Adam who were treated more as gentlemen.

Brown's world: English landscapes

Brown was supremely lucky to come of age at a time when all the circumstances were right for him to change gardens forever. He grasped the opportunity to exercise his landscaping talents at a time of political and economic stability. If he was bold he could make wondrous (and profitable) things out of the advances in both technical and artistic fields.

Improvement was the ultimate Georgian buzzword and landowners were desperate to improve their estates. Not only was the park a long-established sign of aristocratic privilege, it also required that commodity which only the elite had – land in abundance. Land spelt wealth. But the park was not just a work of art like the coveted Claude paintings hanging in the mansions. It was very practical too. It combined leisure and recreation with financial returns: timber, grass (hay and grazing), fish, fowl (shooting) and livestock improvement. Afforestation, enclosure, reclamation and park-making were all embraced as part of this mania for improvement.

Brown's proving ground was at Stowe in Buckinghamshire in the 1740s, when for eight years he worked under the strict supervision of the inspired, even driven, 'amateur' owner-landscaper Lord Cobham. Formality and rigid lines in gardens were long gone, with Lord Cobham having blazed a trail to the informal for the previous 30 years. When Brown started at Stowe he was given his master's last great scheme, the Grecian Valley, to lay out. Although Brown was lent out to advise at country estates owned by Lord Cobham's

LEFT | Landscape parks were at the heart of the Agrarian Revolution (*Thomas Coke, MP for Norfolk, Inspecting Sheep*, Thomas Weaver, late eighteenth century).

friends and relations, it wasn't until 1750 that he was able to start making his mark on the landscapes of the wealthy country-wide as an independent designer. A rural Arcadian landscape became *de rigeur*, and by the 1750s the man of taste with a country estate hankered after this more relaxed style as well as land improvement.

Brown's style was radical. By 1750 the *Spectator*-writer Joseph Addison's exhortations of the 1710s were the coming thing: discard garden formality, abolish parterres, clipped topiary and hedges, and avenues, and instead embrace informal and Arcadian principles. Wealthy British garden makers after the Civil War, from the 1660s to the 1720s, had enthusiastically laid out formal Dutch and French-inspired gardens. But many also kept their hunting parks beyond and enjoyed views over the foreground formality into the wider, untamed landscape. These complex gardens and huge, avenued parks had their drawbacks, taking endless maintenance to remain crisp and presentable. But, particularly in Britain, the undulating (and even mountainous) country estate was not well suited to great unbroken views along vistas framed by avenues and hedges as epitomised by the iconic French designer Le Nôtre at Versailles and Vaux le Vicomte. The endless flatness of parts of France and Holland was much better suited to make spectacular statements of this kind, as rigidly defined landscapes of control, wealth and power.

Artistically, Brown's time had come. Although he didn't originate the English landscape garden he grasped its principles with fervour and used it with

LEFT | William Hogarth's 'serpentine line of beauty', published in 1753, permeated the Georgian world, and was embraced in English landscape parks (*The Analysis of Beauty*, William Hogarth, 1753).

panache. Reaction to the straight line had set in, and thinkers and artists looked towards the reign of Dame Nature, albeit a controlled version. The painter and writer William Hogarth published his *Analysis of Beauty* in 1753, setting out his idea of shapes and forms that were universally pleasing. The 'serpentine line of beauty' was a key concept, and became synonymous with the lines of the landscape park. Serpentine lines were the most acceptable lines of grace and were the underlying principle of beauty. The S curve dominated Georgian ideas in decoration. The philosopher Edmund Burke published his *Inquiry … into the Sublime and Beautiful* in 1757, defining 'beautiful' again in such a way that it was ideally expressed in a landscape park. Horace Walpole claimed the English landscape garden for Britain. England had invented this modern and 'natural' style of garden; it was the garden style of the nation, and it was the culmination of garden design. Nothing could possibly better it. Walpole championed William Kent (who 'leaped the fence and saw that all nature was a garden') and his successor 'Capability' Brown, gleefully dismissing the French formal style as foreign and alien. Brown could adapt this absurdly robust and yet elegant style to any site that presented itself. It was a work of art that was lovely to live in and also made a financial return.

Classical Italy comes to Brown's Britain

The golden age of the Grand Tour of Europe during the Georgian eighteenth century was essentially a very British phenomenon and had a profound effect on country-house owners and their aspirations for their estates. Initially the tour was undertaken by wealthy young men of good family who sometimes spent several years in Europe. Their whole education had revolved around the classical authors and here they could easily relate to the remains and related culture they found. They developed a deep and personal emotional involvement as they eagerly hoovered up antique sculpture and the works of Old Masters as souvenirs and, once home, built galleries for them in their country houses to remind them of their youthful odysseys.

Rome was the goal for those seeking classical culture, and later in the century Greece too. Although the tourists spent time in France, its culture was not held in the same esteem, even though France had had a great effect on British design after the Restoration in 1660. As time went on art professionals such as architect Robert Adam and painter Joshua Reynolds also made the Grand Tour to educate themselves fully.

Access to Europe was relatively easy from the end of the Duke of Marlborough's Wars for Queen Anne (1713) until the 1740s with the War of the Austrian Succession, and then again from 1748 until the French Revolution

(1789). The young, rich Georgian tourists, known in Italy as *milordi*, returned to Britain full of enthusiasm for an idealised past and were keen to evoke it in their own properties. They discussed their aspirations within new private clubs such as the Dilettante and Divan Societies. The influence of Italy and Italian architects, particularly Andrea Palladio (1508–80), himself much influenced by ancient Rome, pervaded the landscape garden. The antique buildings the Grand Tourists all saw were used as models for many houses, and for garden and park buildings, particularly the temples and columns. Holkham in Norfolk, another of Brown's sites, probably demonstrates best the influence of the Grand Tour on the country-house estate.

Most importantly for Brown, the Grand Tourists were captivated by the rural Arcadian landscape of the previous century's painters, Claude and Poussin. Their Arcadia, inspired by the ancient region of classical Greece, evoked rural peace and simplicity. More frighteningly, Salvator Rosa painted rough, wild landscapes of witches, *banditti*, mountains and forests, and these were models for rougher countryside.

Beguiled, the *milordi* returned home determined to evoke the landscape of a mythical calm that reigned in the countryside. This was ideally suited to Brown's talents. Claude and Poussin set poetic classical and biblical scenes in an idealised countryside, usually based on the Roman *campagna*, which was not so different from that at home. The figures, though, were insignificant in the composition compared with the naturalness of these landscapes. Their true subject was the light, atmosphere and poetic mood of the natural world, which were the important things to replicate back at home. Quantities of these paintings were bought, shipped home in crates, and still hang in the stately homes of Britain. As intended in Italy the *milordi* often hung them to complement views over their pastoral idyll outside rather than to focus attention on the scene within the picture frame. More prosaically their pastoral idyll was translated into artistry on the ground by Brown's expertise, and gangs of men via mud and toil. The writer and garden maker Alexander Pope observed, 'all gardening is landscape painting. Just like a landscape hung up'. It remains the ever-varied view through the windows of many country houses, drawing on painterly devices of perspective (foreground, middle ground and distance), grouping, and contrasting light and shade to create the illusion of pure, idealised nature.

The process was epitomised by Tom Stoppard in his play *Arcadia*, 'English landscape was invented by gardeners imitating foreign painters who were evoking classical authors. The whole thing was brought home in the luggage from the Grand Tour.' Essentially it was 'Capability' Brown doing Claude, who was doing Virgil. Arcadia!'

Brown's world: the maelstrom of Georgian Britain

Thrilling changes were afoot in Britain by the 1750s, but, luckily for Brown, they avoided the devastating political upheaval or economic catastrophe that other European countries endured. Instead Brown worked against the backdrop of the Enlightenment, of new ideas, of patrons who looked outwards and drove electrifying change, of phenomenal wealth from Britain's emerging position as a world superpower. It was a time of social and economic transformation. His world was an exciting one.

With political stability at home, combined with great innovations in technology and land ownership as well as artistic sensibility, the time was ripe to make the most of his talents and contacts. Agriculture, transport, irrigation technology and engineering were

BELOW | Engineering developments for drainage and canals helped Brown to create great rivers and lakes in his parks. He collaborated with canal expert James Brindley at Alnwick Castle (Francis Parsons, 1770)

developing in great strides, and there were new trading opportunities, particularly free trade across the North Atlantic and the enormous income from new colonies far afield (largely run on the products of slavery), as well as the East India Company's annexation of India. This gave the elite plenty of disposable income to indulge in large-scale matters of taste on their country estates and country houses, playing at being 'improving' farmers, laying out the English landscape garden and clothing it with the influx of exotic plants arriving from colonies and newly discovered continents.

ABOVE | The Georgian transport boom gave owners easier access to their country estates, improved the economy, and allowed tourism to flourish (*The London to Liverpool Coach*, J. Cordrey, late eighteenth century).

In 1746, the threat of civil war from the Charles Stuart, had finally been stamped out at Culloden after the Jacobite Rising. Britain was at peace internally. Of course, various wars erupted overseas, always with France on the other side, including the Seven Years War (1756–63) involving most of the major powers, and the American War of Independence (1775–83). Happily for Brown these hostilities had little effect on the doings of wealthy landowners at home. By the 1760s Britain had become the world's leading colonial power and the most powerful maritime power.

While politicians steered the country, they still found time to attend to their park-making. The Whig oligarchy that largely ran Georgian Britain associated the English landscape garden with notions of patriotism, liberty and freedom, with a prosperous meritocracy, promoting it as the national style of gardening. They saw its serpentine lines and supposedly unfettered landscape as a reaction against the rigid formality of the great European gardens associated with Absolute Monarchy and Papism. The productive British 'forest' garden was to be preferred to useless artifice. This identifiably native style was elevated to an art form and exported to enthusiastic reception in Europe, Russia and North America.

The economy was booming and the wealthy had the means to create parks. Funds might come from inherited money and estate wealth, or expanding colonial interests underpinned by efforts of the remote work force of the slave trade, or via political sinecures and siphoning public funds, or a combination of these and other sources. Clive of India was the epitome of what a Georgian man could achieve. He annexed India for his country's trade after winning the Battle of Plassey in 1757, trouncing the French forces, and was ennobled for his efforts. In doing so he acquired vast Indian wealth, which he poured into personal projects including Claremont, house and park by Brown.

IMPROVEMENT IN THE AIR

Improvement was racing along in other spheres. In transport, turnpike roads and new steel carriage springs gave greater speed. A noticeable increase in the efficiency of road travel occurred in the 1750s and 1760s. Travel and tourism grew. The canal network was born.

The main roads were improved by turnpike trusts, and engineers such as Telford who laid down better surfaces and gradients. Both Brown, his clients and their guests, were dependent on road transport to reach these country estates, so road improvements meant they could more easily move between their town houses in London and even the remotest country estates between the seasons. With sufficient funds and determination roads could be moved, often as part of land enclosure and turnpiking schemes, away from the country house and the newly laid-out park. Indeed, many parks are still enclosed by eighteenth-century main roads, diverted in a wide arc outside the park from the more convenient straight line past the mansion.

Vehicle design improved in tandem with the roads, but still the main engine was the horse, whether saddle or coach. The number of such horses greatly increased. Landscape parks were ideal to keep horses fed via grazing and hay. Breeding home-grown mares with newly acquired Arab sires led to the Thoroughbred, which is still the classiest and most highly prized of horses. A classic Georgian icon, bred by racing-mad Georgians, the versatile Thoroughbred populates many country-house paintings: think Stubbs, think mares and foals beneath shady trees in a park. More prosaically, lessons from breeding the Thoroughbred informed stock-breeding programmes in the agricultural revolution of the later Georgians.

A British tourist boom resulted. The wealthy went on extended tours in which they visited and wrote about British landscape and country estates, to each other and in print, including comment on Brown's works. Guide books were issued, not just about newly appreciated landscapes like the River Wye in Herefordshire and the Lake District, but also dozens of the greatest mansions and their parks such as Blenheim, Croome and Stowe. The new travellers mapped, illustrated and described the glories of these places, and as they saw his work, Brown's reputation blossomed. One ubiquitous country-house visitor, Mrs Lybbe Powys, reported that over 2,300 people signed the visitors book at Wilton House, Wiltshire in 1775, even before Brown advised there in 1779.

Countryside was invented as a civilised concept at this time. Brown's career coincided with the first 'wave' of parliamentary enclosure of farmland, between 1750 and 1780. This rather dry reorganisation of land ownership was key to park-making and sometimes aroused much protest from small landowners who felt they were losing out. It was particularly focused on the Midland counties, one of the main centres of Brown's commissions. Land previously farmed as clusters of strips was consolidated into large areas that could now be laid out as a single park by wealthy

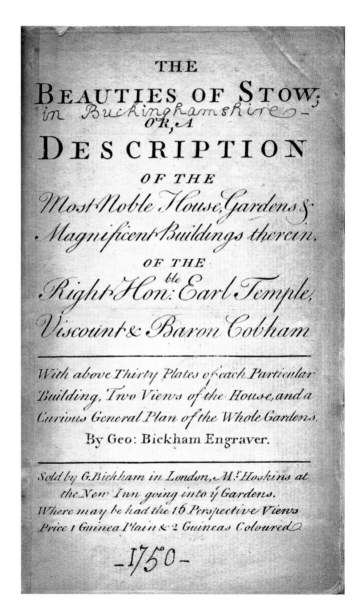

owners who had the means and contacts to sponsor Parliamentary Enclosure Acts. The old open field systems in which many people held strips all over the parish and rights over common land were abolished and the small owners supposedly compensated or given blocks of land.

The great landowners could now indulge in a united vision for their newly consolidated hundreds of acres. Richard Grenville's election to Parliament (he was later Earl Temple and inherited Stowe) enabled him to engineer an Enclosure Act at his family estate at Wotton Underwood in Buckinghamshire in 1743. This gave him the hundreds of acres in a single block where he could indulge his landscaping ambitions via Brown over the next two decades.

Agricultural husbandry and breeding, both stock and crops, developed greatly as the Agrarian Revolution gathered pace. The husbandry of hay and pasture was improved, important with the increasing use of the horse for transport and recreation. A park dotted around with clumps and specimen trees could only be used for pasture or hay, not arable crops that required land to be ploughed, demonstrating how wealthy a landowner was who did not need to rely on such crops for income. Woodland cultivation became a country landowner's preoccupation, with prizes offered for good examples to encourage others.

Public roads and footpaths might be closed or diverted when parks were created. When the catalyst was the Enclosure Act, making large areas of land available, new roads were made, enabling the owner to move the public road away from the house to a distant line beyond the new park. We often arrive at a park entrance and have to turn sharp right or left to skirt the park. This is probably because the old direct road was used for the drive to the mansion, and when the park was laid out the public route was diverted to a new, circuitous line. Perimeter belts provided seclusion and privacy from public roads, with lodges and gates.

In country-house architecture the heavy Palladian classical style was ousted by not just its natural successor, the more elegant Neo-classical style, but also by the medieval Gothic, according to the client's taste. Many an old manor house was completely rebuilt on a new site or, less expensively, refaced, or a new site was chosen for a fashionable new mansion unencumbered by the clutter and squalor of a village at its feet. Some villages were demolished to make way for Brown's parks and rebuilt as planned model villages for the tenants. Cottagers were moved to new villages outside the parks at Milton Abbey, Dorset, and Nuneham Courtenay, Oxfordshire, so that the landscapes of these patrons of the arts could be made to look like a Claude painting. Other villages had gradually declined

BELOW | Highly bred horses were important and prestigious in the park, which fed and housed them (*Five Brood Mares at the Duke of Cumberland's Stud Farm in Windsor Great Park*, George Stubbs, 1765).

and the settlements vanished, so with little effort the inhabitants were rehoused to make way for the now-iconic rolling park lawns.

Sport was essential in the country estate, especially with major developments in hunting and shooting. The park was ideal as a game larder with its open pasture, copses and woodland. Enclosures allowed large areas of agricultural land to be hunted with hounds, either for the traditional hares or, a new target, foxes. Park copses were not only ornamental but acted as coverts. The new Thoroughbred was ideal not just for racing but for hunting too.

Game Acts protected birds owned by the landed rich, and imposed hugely punitive penalties for poachers, including hanging. Guns became lighter and more accurate and pheasants became the bird of choice to shoot, for the challenge they posed when flying. Pheasants roost at the edges of woodland with easy access to fields, edges ideally provided by long narrow sheltering and screening belts, woodland and copses, integral to the landscape park.

Breeding birds and game keeping became more organised. These were new tasks for staff, needing to keep up stocks against the new guns that were so effective that one hunter complained that 'few fowls escape'. John Byng, visiting Blenheim in 1787, found that such numbers of birds were hatched and reared that he almost trod on them in the grass.

Brown as Georgian Man – 'more than genius'

Into this maelstrom of Georgian Britain, Brown, with his enormous professional confidence, very quickly fashioned a business niche for himself, with little serious competition. Here, unlike in mainland Europe, the conditions were perfect for self-made men with drive to succeed without royal patronage. Brown is a shining example: he was a great artist, but he was also an engineer and serious businessman, an extraordinary coinciding of talents and skills. His genial personality cemented his success with clients, and he was renowned for his uncommon honesty. In this respect he was a Georgian phenomenon, obtaining his huge success by making the best of his opportunities without resorting to corruption.

EARLY DAYS AND LEARNING HIS TRADE

Lancelot Brown was born in 1716 in the tiny and remote Northumberland village of Kirkharle. His family were of yeoman stock, of a level of respectable standing, and he was schooled to a fair standard at nearby Cambo. His brothers John and George married into local gentry.

OPPOSITE | Hunting foxes across the landscape park with one's own pack of hounds was a new pastime for owners and their guests (*Noel Hill, 1st Lord of Berwick on a Horse with Hounds*, attributed to John Boultbee, c.1780).

LEFT | The English landscape park was ideal for developing the sport of shooting (Samuel Jones, c.1820).

In 1732 the young Lancelot was taken on by the local landowner of Kirkharle, William Loraine, to work on his estate. Here he learnt the skills of improving the land with horticulture, husbandry and land reclamation. Brown left Northumberland for the south in 1739. What he did for the next two years is not known. Perhaps he worked on landscapes at Kiddington, Oxfordshire, and quite likely in Lincolnshire. Nothing is known of his life until in 1741 he came out of the shadows. He hit gold when he went to work as head gardener for Lord Cobham, one of the greatest landscape makers and garden visionaries of the era.

The capable Northumbrian arrived at Stowe in far north Buckinghamshire in early 1741. He grasped a major position in the most renowned and influential garden in Britain and Europe. He soon became more than just head gardener, and was given the extensive building works in the house and grounds to manage too. This was his formative period during which he consolidated the skills and artistic eye necessary for his forthcoming independent career.

Lord Cobham's visionary garden was nearly complete except for the final piece in the jigsaw, the sweeping Grecian Valley headed by a giant Greek temple reminiscent of the Acropolis in Athens. Brown at the tender age of 25 took on a vast and complex garden as well as some 40 men to do this, executing testing new schemes for Lord Cobham in his last, eight-year-long, garden-making phase. Lancelot's integrity led to him becoming virtually clerk of works for the great works in the house, garden buildings and grounds that

LEFT | Kirkharle church where Brown was baptised in 1716.

RIGHT | Brown's first family home at Stowe, after he married Bridget (Biddy) in 1744, was in one of the imposing pair of Boycott Pavilions where they lived with their growing family until 1751.

were in a perpetual state of flux. He followed in the footsteps of the foremost exponent of the naturalistic landscape, William Kent, who designed the Elysian Fields at Stowe in the 1730s.

At Stowe, under Lord Cobham's eye, Brown abolished Bridgeman's Frenchified parterre below the house, laid out his own master work, the Grecian Valley, altered the lakes and planted thousands of trees. To create the curved bowl of the Grecian Valley 18,350m³ (24,000 yards³) of earth and subsoil had to be carved out of the virgin scrubland, laboriously using spade and barrow and horse-drawn cart. Even with his engineering expertise it failed as the intended lake and became a great grassy amphitheatre surrounded by exotic buildings and sculpture linked by shrubbery-lined perimeter walks. He built the monument erected to Lord Cobham by his wife in the form of a giant Roman column, 30.5m (100ft) high. He supervised building work in the house as well as the erection of the stables and coach houses and some of the greatest of Cobham's garden buildings, designed by James Gibbs: the Gothic and Lady's Temples and Palladian Bridge.

Lord Cobham was a true patron. He had a double success in launching Brown as a landscape gardener and William Pitt (Pitt the Elder) as a politician, both to become masters of Georgian Britain in their respective fields. Quite early on, Cobham lent Brown to several of his friends and family including his brother at Wotton Underwood some 15 miles south, and his friends Lord and Lady Denbigh at Newnham Paddox in Warwickshire in 1745. This was the start of the web of contacts that was to benefit Brown for the rest of his career.

BELOW | At Stowe church in 1742 Bridget Wayett, a Lincolnshire alderman's daughter, married Northumbrian Brown. Here they baptised four children and buried one before they left in 1751.

Family life was conventional, with no whiff of public scandal. On 22 November 1744 he married Bridget Wayet from Boston, Lincolnshire, perhaps having met her there during his 'lost' two years before Stowe. Her family were surveyors and engineers, her father an alderman of Boston, and landowner. Lancelot and Bridget (affectionately called Biddy) married by licence in the little Stowe parish church. This was the last vestige of the lost village, its valley remodelled by Cobham as Kent's Elysian Fields in the 1730s, his sublime and innovative essay in the Picturesque. The church, still a parish church, remains hidden in garden trees, its presence unsuspected unless you know where to look. It was never a feature of Cobham's

great landscape scheme, he just hid it with trees and shrubbery. In 1746 Bridget was born to the newlyweds, the first of four children born here, and christened on 11 October. Their eldest son, also Lancelot but known as Lance, was christened on 13 January 1748. William was christened in April 1750 but survived only a month and was buried on 14 May, but their fourth child, John, was christened in April 1751 and went on to become an admiral. They lived at Stowe until late in 1751 in one of the pair of huge Boycott Pavilions, out in the park marking the old entrance to the main drive to the mansion. His family became the bedrock of his life to whom he returned from his arduous journeys time and again to recover his health.

As well as achieving personal milestones, Brown was educating himself in the more refined areas of his professional life. He copied out a 15-page glossary from the *Builder's Dictionary*, published in 1734, and by 1747 was competent to draw building plans. His landscape drawings were influenced by the style of Kent, with whom he was lucky enough to overlap at Stowe. Kent was a good role model as he was of similar social background: a lad from Bridlington who grasped opportunities, was taken up by his patron Lord Burlington and worked extensively on both buildings and landscapes for the wealthy and powerful from the 1720s until he died in 1748.

BROWN LAUNCHED!

When Lord Cobham died in 1749, Brown sensed his opportunity. He could have run his own business in tandem with his position as head gardener at Stowe, working for Cobham's successor, his nephew Earl Temple. Instead he took the plunge and got stuck into extensive and challenging jobs as a freelance designer and landscaper. One of the first was his greatest early creation from scratch, Croome, Worcestershire, rebuilding the house and stables and making a park out of the surrounding great boggy landscape. Luckily he met the gentleman architect Sanderson Miller, just as he was considering his future beyond Stowe, and benefited from Miller's friendship and recommendations. Miller probably introduced Brown to the Earl of Coventry just as he needed a capable man to fulfil his vast vision for Croome. Brown also landed the contract for Warwick Castle Park *c*.1749–50 for Lord Brooke, later the Earl of Warwick. Walpole noted with faint praise at the time that it was 'well laid out by one Brown who has set up on a few ideas of Kent and Mr Southcote'. It was clearly in the coming fashionable style, as Walpole continued that 'little Brooke … has submitted to let his garden and park be natural.' The critical Walpole watched Brown's career and style blossom, and became a confirmed fan.

In autumn 1751 Brown, aged 35, left the security of Stowe for the life of a freelance designer and landscaper, taking the family to live in Hammersmith Mall, London. Usefully the area was littered with Thameside nurseries, but he also fell into a lively world, in which the Thames upstream from London was mushrooming with aristocratic villas. Brown joined the artistic community there: Horace Walpole (a very influential contact) at Strawberry Hill, and poet Owen Cambridge in Twickenham, plus many self-made men: artist William Hogarth, and the playwright and actor-manager David Garrick who lived at Hampton, and others. He belonged to the Royal Society for the Encouragement of Arts, Manufactures and Commerce (formed 1754), which interested itself in social and economic matters. These extended to promoting interest in the improvement of greensward by giving awards to nurserymen for good dressed seed and to offering prizes for model forestry schemes. His friend Garrick poked gentle fun at him occasionally in his plays, with reference to 'fine capabilities' and the rules of taste to be followed. Brown also knew the great botanist and explorer Joseph Banks, promoter of Kew Gardens, which thanks to his efforts became the centre of a worldwide network of colonial botanical gardens.

Sadly, the Browns' fourth son, born in 1754, died shortly afterwards, and a daughter, Anne, was born and died in 1756. The last two children were,

TOP LEFT | Viscount Cobham, of Stowe, Bucks, was Brown's first major patron for whom he was head gardener from 1741 (Jean-Baptiste Van Loo, c.1700).

TOP RIGHT | The 6th Earl of Coventry of Croome, Worcestershire, was Brown's greatest patron from the start of his independent career. They remained firm friends for over 30 years until Brown's death (Allan Ramsay, 1764).

BOTTOM LEFT | William Pitt, 1st Earl of Chatham (Pitt the Elder), Prime Minister and outstanding politician, was another devoted patron of Brown's. Both were masters of Georgian Britain in their respective fields (after Richard Brompton, c.1734).

BOTTOM RIGHT | Sanderson Miller was a gentleman architect at the heart of a network of rich landowners to whom he introduced Brown early on in his practice (Thomas Hudson, c.1750).

however, survivors. Margaret (known as Peggy) was born in 1758 and Thomas in 1761. The children became a credit to their parents. None of Brown's sons followed him into his business, but perhaps this is what he and Biddy had planned, given his financial success and social connections. Instead they moved up the social ladder to join the Establishment. With business booming, Lance was sent to Eton in 1761, among the offspring of his father's clients. Eton, with Westminster, educated by far the majority of powerful Georgians and here he was swiftly dubbed Capey by his schoolfellows, a sign that his father was clearly well-known in these circles.

Eton was the first strategic step for Lance on the social and political ladder, for after law studies at Lincoln's Inn, in 1774 he was encouraged to put up for Parliament for Cockermouth. There was some skullduggery from his patron Sir William Lowther, whom his father had advised at Lowther Hall in the 1760s, so that the son had to wait another six years before fulfilling his parliamentary ambitions, as Member for Totnes. His father had to wait until 1780 to be paid for advice and plans given in 1763 by his client who was described as a 'madman too influential to be locked up'. Lance sat in Parliament several times and became in 1795 a Gentleman of the King's Privy Chamber. John went into the navy, becoming an Admiral of the Blue, and Thomas entered the Church. Bridget married the architect son of Brown's Hammersmith neighbour and colleague builder Henry Holland, taking a £5,000 dowry with her. Henry junior prospered after a springboard start in a loose partnership with his father-in-law, taking on his major building projects from the 1770s and building up his own practice.

Brown had an outstanding CV: a firm grounding during his decade at Stowe, then Croome as his initial freelance master work, both shouting not just his expertise but the confidence with which great and educated men were willing to endow him. It should be said that Brown was probably not allowed his head by either Lord Cobham or Lord Coventry, but was heavily steered by them. They were opinionated men with a (justifiably) high regard for their own taste and would have dominated Brown's creativity in their own grounds. Even so, their patronage and promotion led others to invest confidence

BELOW | Bridget, the Browns' eldest daughter, married architect Henry Holland who worked closely with Brown later in his career (John Hoppner).

(as well as large sums) in him and his career never faltered. Prime Minister Pitt the Elder told Lady Stanhope that she could take no other advice 'so intelligent or more honest' than Brown's.

Brown combined landscaping and architecture as part of an inseparable artistic masterpiece. It was the embodiment of a landscape painting with every brushstroke carefully considered, but for real, not just in an image. The country house was at the heart of the landscape design, with garden buildings as focal points linked by paths, and views framed by expert planting. He provided various levels of services, ranging from a simple survey charting the grounds as they were, leading to a design, and on to a full-blown selection of designs that he would supervise being laid out either by the owner's staff or himself, often taking some years. A decade of involvement was not uncommon on the larger schemes. The sum of 31 guineas would give you a visit or two and a site survey; £100 bought a design. After that the sky was the limit, up to tens of thousands of pounds.

Throughout his career Brown employed a team of assistant surveyors and landscapers to map the ground and implement his schemes. Williamson the London nurseryman supplied many of his plants throughout his career. After he obtained his royal post at Hampton Court in 1764 he took on his two most longstanding assistants, Samuel Lapidge and Jonathan Spyers. Lapidge was his office manager, keeping the accounts, including the account book from the 1760s to his death in 1783, which survives in the Royal Horticultural Society's Lindley Library in Vincent Square, London. Lapidge drafted plans and was finally Brown's executor.

In 1753 Brown put everything on a more formal footing when he opened a bank account. He chose Drummond's Bank, noted for the number of artists and craftsmen on its books. 'Old Andrew' Drummond's clients included cabinet-maker Chippendale, painter Thomas Gainsborough, sculptor Henry Cheere, plasterer Joseph Rose, architects Sir William Chambers and latterly Brown's son-in-law Henry Holland. Later on Brown worked for the Drummonds in Hampshire, laying out a park and pleasure ground at Cadland near Fawley. Bankers, although strictly speaking 'in trade', were also men of taste and some were prolific garden-makers, including Henry Hoare at Stourhead, an allegorical garden to rival Stowe. Drummond's Bank account books, along with Brown's own account book, paint a picture of his extraordinarily productive career and range of clients. He was constantly touring England and Wales for the next 30 years between the country estates of wealthy and powerful men, with occasional forays into Wales and advice on schemes further afield.

ROYAL GARDENER AT LAST

A royal post eluded Brown for a surprisingly long time, given his early renown. Even a dozen and more of the Great and the Good could not succeed initially in a petition submitted in 1758 to gain him a royal appointment, signed by two dukes, 11 other peers and one commoner, including many of Brown's patrons. The man with the patronage for the post of Royal Gardener, the Duke of Newcastle, was no fan of Brown it seems and did not deal with the petition for three years, before offering the post to someone else. However, a second petition proved successful in 1764 when Brown became Master Gardener at His Majesty's Gardens and Waters at Hampton Court. He also took on St James's in London.

Now the Brown family moved from Hammersmith to the lovely red-brick Wilderness House in the gardens of Hampton Court, overlooking the famous maze, where they lived until Brown's death in 1783. A 'wilderness' was not, as we might think today, an unkempt bramble patch, but the opposite – a designed woodland shrubbery of horticultural delights with paths through it, linking garden buildings and views containing interesting plants, in which to wander or pause and drink in the sensuousness of it all.

ABOVE | Hampton Court where Brown became Royal Gardener for George III in 1764. He left the outdated geometric garden untouched, saying that his 'good sense and honesty' led him not to change it to his preferred taste 'out of respect to himself and his profession' (Leonard Knyff, c.1702).

Once in that coveted royal position Brown made the most of it. He managed the royal grounds, with the annual lump sum of around £2,000, paying the gardeners and buying materials to maintain the gardens as per the past 50 years. His account book records quarterly payments of £500. This probably left him a comfortable profit. But its formal lines and great avenues remained frozen in time. He was quoted as saying that this 'good sense and honesty' to decline to change it to his preferred taste was 'out of respect to himself and his profession'. More likely this preservation was because the royal interest was elsewhere and no funds were forthcoming. He did, however, stop clipping the topiary so that the yews and hollies grew out of their strictly corsetted shapes. He also planted the Great Vine, a prolific Black Hamburg that still flourishes in a glasshouse.

Brown could carry on his consultancy, but he needed to set up an office and yard as his practice flourished. Here he based his assistants Spyers and Lapidge, and continued his phenomenally successful career, leaping the fences and flinging wide the park views of England.

Even with his royal position and patronage from the greatest politicians of the day he never acquired a title, not even a lowly knighthood. This was no different to other great Georgian landscape artists and architects: Royal Gardener Charles Bridgeman, William Kent and, after Brown, Humphry Repton; even Robert Adam was never knighted, although his immediate rival William Chambers obtained a knighthood by a back-door method via Sweden. Despite the gardeners' prowess and effect on their patrons' worlds they remained players not gentlemen.

OPPOSITE | Brown's Black Hamburg Great Vine at Hampton Court is said to be the largest grape vine in the world and is still prolific.

LEFT | Brown bought the Manor House, Fenstanton near Huntingdon, in 1768 for £13,000, which came with the Lordship of the Manor and an agricultural estate. He never moved in and his family home remained at Hampton Court.

LORD OF THE MANOR

The Lordship of the Manor of Fenstanton, in the little East Anglian county of Huntingdonshire, was Brown's main social and financial acquisition, in 1768. For this, including two manor houses, he paid £13,000 to Lord Northampton of Castle Ashby where he was working (some £1m equivalent today). Its value was not so much in the buildings as in the vast amount of land – 2,668 acres – that came with it around two sleepy, flatly watery villages. The attractive little manor house was the size of a modest farmhouse, nothing pretentious, but he bought apple trees for its orchard, two of which survive. A landed property of his own offered security for his family while in a tied house at Hampton Court and somewhere to retire eventually. This also gave him the standing for his name to be put up as High Sheriff of Huntingdonshire, as which he served from 1770 to 1771. The post was fitting for minor gentry or upcoming men of business, and it seems that Lance, aged 22, probably took on most of the tasks, starting him on his own political road. The manor stayed in the family for over 100 years until it was sold in lots in the 1870s and 80s.

Fenstanton was perhaps an enigmatic choice and somewhere that Brown had no obvious connection with. The owner, Lord Northampton, was keen to sell as he had a financial crisis looming, including debts to Brown for considerable work carried out at Castle Ashby. This was Brown's most frantic decade of work, and he needed something to invest the dividends in. Perhaps the answer to the choice of place lies in rumour: that in the 1750s he had an illegitimate daughter, Mary Elizabeth Cowling. Maybe she was connected with his 25 years 'of happiness' advising at Burghley, as he referred to it. Fenstanton lay conveniently on the way to Burghley, quietly obscure and remote from his business in London and family in Hampton Court. Lancelot senior never set up his family home there nor attempted seriously to 'improve' either the manor house or landscape. Indeed Biddy and the family apparently never even stayed there. However, Mary Elizabeth lived in Fenstanton and was, it seems, buried in the vault in the church there with the Browns.

Brown acquired a coat of arms surmounted by a griffon's head. The shield was wreathed in flowers and foliage with the Roman Cicero's Latin motto *Nunquam minus solus, quam cum solus* translated as 'Never less alone than when wholly alone'. Given Lancelot's firm Christian faith this could have been interpreted as 'A Christian is never less alone than when alone.'

BROWN'S PERSONAL LEGACY

Brown died after a night out at Lord Coventry's on 6th February 1783, when he collapsed on the way home to his daughter's home. He was buried at Fenstanton, later joined by his wife and two eldest sons. A quirky Gothic wall panel in the chancel enjoys a fitting epitaph by the renowned poet William Mason who conveyed Brown's great virtues:

> Ye sons of Elegance, who truly taste
> The Simple charms that genuine Art supplies,
> Come from the sylvan Scenes His Genius grac'd
> And offer here your tributary Sighs.
> But know that more than Genius slumbers here,
> Virtues were his which Arts best power transcend.
> Come, ye superior train who these revere
> And weep the Christian Husband, Father, Friend.

The value of Brown's estate must have been considerable. He left enough property in Lincolnshire, Huntingdonshire and Cambridgeshire to provide for Biddy his wife an annuity of £400 a year, as well as £1,000 cash, his personal effects, the household goods, horses and 'chariot'. He had previously bestowed £5,000 on his daughter Bridget when she married Henry Holland in 1773, and he left substantial bequests to her and to his other children. Lance had £7,000 and all his father's instruments; Bridget had a further

LEFT | Brown's memorial in Fenstanton church. After Brown's death it was said that 'Lady Nature's second husband, is dead!' The King said to one of Brown's foremen at Kew, 'Brown is dead. Now Mellicant, you and I can do here what we please'.

£1,000 and a flat silver candlestick as token of his 'unchangeable affection'; his second son, the budding admiral John, received £2,500; while the youngsters Margaret and Thomas had £6,000 apiece. Various small bequests were made to servants, friends and relatives. His business executor was the faithful Lapidge who was given 100 guineas for this service. The total value in cash and property he left may have exceeded £40,000, in today's terms several million pounds, perhaps more, not bad for a yeoman's son – but he had worked himself to death for it. Biddy went to live in Kensington and their family prospered on the foundation he had laid for them in the professions.

LANCELOT THE MAN

What are we to make of Lancelot's life? He was the epitome of a Georgian entrepreneur, a man for whom all the circumstances were propitious to succeed in business if he had the ability. Added to this was the genius of his 'poet's feeling and painter's eye' (William Mason, *The English Garden*). He had the skills and capability to make the most of his circumstances, but unlike many others did not indulge in sharp practices. This was surely the combination of innate honesty and sound understanding that his reputation rested on.

Professionally he was a driven man, but in his home life his contemporaries had no mud to sling at him. His was a happy family life, marred by bouts of illness, but he got up and out and back in the saddle as soon as he could. His surviving correspondence is witness to how dearly he loved his wife and children. Personally, his company was enjoyed by many of the highest in the land but he never became one of them, and for relaxation he would return to his family and his close friends around Hampton Court.

And what of the wealth he amassed after all this adulation and sheer hard work? The sum he left, although substantial, did not reflect the huge sums that had gone through his books over the years, much of which went to pay others who worked for him. This reflected his unending hard work, honesty and fairness, and the fervour of the greatest in the land to commission works of art by that genius, the Omnipotent Magician.

RIGHT | Brown's circle of artistic friends around Hampton Court included the famous actor-manager David Garrick, who wrote of him 'I envy his genius, yet doat on ye Man' (*David Garrick and his Wife by his Temple to Shakespeare at Hampton*, Johann Zoffany c.1762).

CHAPTER 2

Brown's ABC: art, business and clients

Brown's business

Phenomenal is the only word for 'Capability' Brown's client portfolio. It reads like a roll-call of the wealthiest and most powerful men (and a few women too) of the Georgian Augustan Age, on both sides of the political divide: peers, MPs and laymen.

Think of Blenheim, Croome, Petworth, Alnwick, Brocklesby, Harewood, Luton Hoo, Milton Abbey, Wimpole, Bowood, Longleat, Audley End, Ashridge, and beyond – the list of stunners goes on and on. Pitt the Elder reported that Brown shared 'the private hours' of the king, dined 'familiarly with his neighbour of Sion' (the Duke of Northumberland) and sat down at the tables 'of all the House of Lords' (perhaps a slight exaggeration). All this success did not turn his head, however. He did not court celebrity, shunned the glamour of society, and there is no whiff of financial, political or sexual scandal, so prevalent among his clients.

Touched by artistic genius and being the polymath he was, Brown was also a skilful entrepreneur with exceptional business acumen. To this he added phenomenal networking skills to take advantage of contacts and win the trust of the aristocracy and major politicians including six British prime

PREVIOUS PAGE | Petworth, Sussex, was one of Brown's early masterpieces. Again he removed complex formal gardens in front of the house and swept the lawns up to the windows.

BELOW | At Blenheim Palace, Oxfordshire, Brown transformed the fussy French-style geometric parterre into a vast lawn. A 40-acre lake replaced the narrow canal, but the endless straight avenue and Vanbrugh's bridge remained at the heart of the park.

ministers. He quickly developed his business to a vast scale and he worked relentlessly during his long and prolific career as a freelance landscape designer over the course of 33 years. Without Brown's connections no one, however talented, could compete with him.

We can track his success from the beginning. Even in his first decade as a freelancer in the 1750s he took on over 40 large commissions and his annual turnover was in the thousands, with over £10,000 in 1759. Business never seriously flagged but continued at this scale and frantic level. Working on 250 or more places, to varying degrees, his masterpieces are well-known. More than 100 giants still display his excellence for our delectation. He is also a legendary character, with much myth surrounding the full extent of his commissions. Brown's alleged presence in a park enhances its interest and value. With his reputation for countrywide coverage, many people have attributed their parks to him on hearsay only.

Detecting Brown

We may never be able to detect all the places where Brown worked. Of course we know his giants, and have probably pinned down most of his lesser jobs, but there are still some unanswered questions. He was no literary man, nor did he have to market himself, for his reputation was spread by word of mouth. Unlike his architectural competitors, including the Adam brothers, he published no books, did not publicise his work or ideas, nor did he leave a diary or an extensive body of letters. However over 100 of his plans and drawings survive, even if not all in his own hand.

BELOW | Berrington Hall, Herefordshire, one of Brown's 'sylvan scenes' that 'His Genius grac'd' with carefully arranged parkland, clumps and specimen trees, water and woodland.

His business paperwork gives us the most obvious clues. His single surviving business account book, started in the 1760s, together with his Drummond's Bank account ledgers from 1753, identify many commissions. They miss his earliest career, and are not even a complete record of all his commissions and transactions in the period they cover. They are very dry documents with little hinting at the exciting details of layouts and schemes. For these we have to look at his design plans and contracts, few of which survive. Formal contracts were drawn up in some detail, specifying the features to be removed and the new works, sometimes including planting. Some of these survive in estate records.

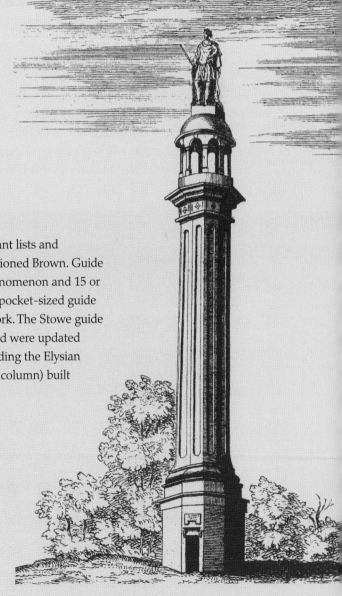

Petworth was one of Brown's early large-scale commissions, with five contracts between 1753 and 1765 worth £5,500. A five-part agreement was made at Charlecote (1760), others survive for Audley End (1763) and Sherborne Castle (1776). The contract at Audley End covered areas that Sir John Griffin did not own, but wanted to acquire. At Burton Constable the owner's notes for discussion survive, alongside detailed minutes of discussions between Brown and the agent, 1772–82. At Tottenham we have notes of Brown's suggestions.

Other sources offer clues, via letters, descriptions, plant lists and accounts in the estate records of those who commissioned Brown. Guide books can be revealing. Tourism was a Georgian phenomenon and 15 or 20 of the great country houses had their own handy pocket-sized guide books, some providing essential detail of Brown's work. The Stowe guide books by Benton Seeley were first printed in 1744 and were updated frequently, eventually reporting Brown's works including the Elysian Fields and illustrating Lord Cobham's Monument (a column) built by Brown, as well as many other buildings.

William Dean's 1824 guide book for Croome is a mine of information; although published over 40 years after Brown's death, little of his work had been altered. William Mavor's 1817 guide book to the park at Blenheim explained Brown's changing sequence of landscape compositions specifically for the casual tourist.

His schemes were painterly just when landscape painting in Britain was blossoming as a genre. Many of the great landscape painters, such as Thomas Hearne, Paul Sandby, Canaletto, Richard Wilson and William Tomkins, recorded them, particularly for proud owners. Pictures of his landscapes even went to Russia, to passionate Anglophile Catherine the Great on her Wedgwood Green Frog dinner service of over 900 pieces. Brown's work at Wimpole and Milton Abbey was displayed on various pieces in up-to-the-minute pictures, but Blenheim was represented by out-of-date pictures before Brown had worked his magic.

Sometimes we have only tenuous scraps where sources are not clear or perhaps are unreliable. His commission at Kiddington is one such likely myth, said to be laid out by him very early in his career c.1740, aged only 24, before he went to Stowe. This is undocumented except as noted by

John Penn in 1813, some 70 years later. Similarly, Gunnersbury near Kew was attributed to Brown by a later owner, Alexander Copland, in the 1830s. He wrote in his memorandum book merely that 'The Grounds were laid out by Mr Brown' in 1754. Nothing else is known to connect Brown to Gunnersbury, but Copland had personal connections with Brown's descendants, and may possibly have known Brown in his latter years.

Where even hearsay fails to connect Brown with a landscape park it is very difficult to attribute it to him (or any other designer) solely on style and appearance. Designers used a similar palette of design elements, but these were applied uniquely depending on the circumstances of the site, although Brown's use of these was usually the most adept. A 'signature' feature is almost impossible to attribute to a particular person and no designer could use a signature feature at every site. Having said this, the presence of one or a few enormous plane trees as strategic specimens, particularly near bridges and water, may be an indicator of Brown's hand, as they are seldom if ever found in parks by his competitors. Plenty of his parks do not have them though. Added to this confusion, the later hand of man and natural attrition in planting and layout have wrought major changes to some of his works.

BELOW | A rare perspective drawing of Brown's vision forms part of the suite of drawings from the 1760s for Blenheim Palace, Oxfordshire. The young landscape iv s framed by Woodstock town, intended to be walled like a medieval town.

Finding work

Finding work was never a problem and, extraordinarily, Brown never had to advertise his services. Throughout his career he returned to the same counties and regions over and over again, called in by many different clients as their circumstances allowed. Generally the owner's cash prosperity was the driver, combined his interest in the project. The wealthiest families had more than one country house and some, such as Lord Bute, commissioned Brown to work on more than one park.

Brown's early connection with Stowe brought him in the 1750s the extensive commission for Wotton Underwood some 15 miles to the south. This was Earl Temple's house before he inherited Stowe from his uncle Lord Cobham. Here for Earl Temple's brother George Grenville, under his brother-in-law Pitt's guidance and inspiration, Brown created in his masterpiece of water engineering an enchanting 2 miles of water scenery. The Dukes of Marlborough of Blenheim owned the more modest Langley Park on the main road to London from Oxford, and Brown was called in to both in the 1760s. The Dukes of Northumberland had Syon Park on the Thames, west of London, convenient for politics and business in London and Windsor, and their huge agricultural estate at Alnwick in remote Northumberland. Brown created masterpieces at both. Likewise Lord Shelburne commissioned Brown at his main country house Bowood, Wiltshire, in the 1760s and then for the park that became Wycombe Abbey in High Wycombe. Lord Bute, a renowned plantsman, called Brown to his estate at Luton Hoo, Bedfordshire, and his marine villa at Highcliffe on the cliffs above Christchurch Bay, Hampshire, and his son employed Brown and architect son-in-law Henry Holland at Cardiff Castle. Brown was lucky he was not required at the Earl's estate Mount Stuart on the Isle of Bute in Scotland.

The easy relationship with most clients was exemplified when Brown wrote in December 1775 from Luton to his wife Biddy. 'I stay'd with Lord Bute two nights and each Day we drank a bottle of Toka[y] wine which was rather too much for me as my cough has been very troublesome'. However, he would express firm opinions when directing works on site: the agent at Tottenham Park writing of a visit by Brown to inspect the works in 1765, remarked wryly that 'If the high bank and trees had been taken down, great would have been the fall indeed, Brown would have excommunicated us all.'

Brown was not infallible. To the owner of Tottenham, Lord Bruce, Brown directly justified his failure to fix a quotation, saying that in doing so 'I should be very sorry to diminish my friends, and very sorry to increase my business, for I have so much to do that it neither answers for profit nor pleasure, for

when I am galloping in one part of the world my men are making blunders and neglects which [make] it very unpleas't.'

Son-in-law, Henry Holland, summed it up: 'No man that I ever met with understood so well what was necessary for the habitation of all ranks and degrees of society; no one ... so well provided for the approach, for the drainage and for the comfort and conveniences of every part of a place he was concerned in. This he did without ever having had one single difference or dispute with any of his employers.' Holland, clearly a distinctly biased observer, added: 'He left them pleased and they remained so as long as he lived.'

Despite this general adulation, some disagreements and tensions were inevitable, usually arising from the self-imposed workload and subsequent delays in visits, but his honesty was never questioned. The most well-known

OPPOSITE | The park at Audley End, Essex, is one of Brown's beauties, but its owner, Sir John Griffin Griffin, was a rare client who disputed Brown's bill.

disagreement was with Sir John Griffin Griffin of Audley End, Essex, in 1765. Delays occurred and an error in executing the lake from the widened River Cam was not rectified to his satisfaction. Sir John refused to pay an outstanding bill. Brown wrote to Sir John that he considered himself 'not honourably treated' but would not pursue the matter. Despite this, Audley End is a fine tribute to Brown's artistry and his reputation did not suffer.

More dramatic was the resolution during a personal confrontation at Branches, Suffolk, also in 1765. The owner, Mr Dickens, refused to pay a disputed bill for £58 and tensions escalated. In Brown's account book it was noted that 'Mr Brown could not get the money for the Extra Work and tore the account before Mr Dickens face and said his say upon that Business to him'. Clearly Mr Brown did occasionally let rip.

Ill health troubled Brown from time to time, particularly asthma, sometimes brought on by his extensive travel on horseback, but he did not spare himself unless prostrated. He was not afraid to mention his indispositions to his clients in correspondence. Lord Arundell wanted him at Wardour Castle, Wiltshire, in 1773, but was resigned to having to wait following a bout of ill health, warmly writing, 'I am very sorry to hear of yr. indisposition and that it prevented me ye pleasure of seeing you here, which I have long wished for...'.

His places and people

Commissions came from pretty much all over England and Brown seldom turned down work. The 250 and more parks he is connected with are sprinkled over a huge countrywide swathe between Exeter and Alnwick and in Wales too. On horseback he sometimes travelled up to 75 miles in a day.

The sequence of his commissions was generally a random result of the circumstances of his clients, often of a recent change in ownership and finances. Some commissions were from landed grandees who had just inherited an estate and wealth to 'improve' it in fashionable style, as happened to the Earls of Coventry and Egremont at Croome and Petworth, and the Lucy family, in residence at Charlecote since the twelfth century.

In the body of England his commissions are sprinkled fairly evenly. Concentrations occur around London and the Home Counties, particularly along the Thames Valley, the West Midlands, in Yorkshire and in Somerset/Wiltshire/Dorset/Hampshire. He rarely travelled to the far West Country, with only four or so commissions clustered in Devon near the balmy coast south of Exeter and nothing in remote Cornwall. Little happened in North Yorkshire

and beyond, but his most notable northerly commissions were a little cluster to the north-east in Northumberland, with Sir Walter Calverley Blackett's Wallington and Rothley Lakes near his home village of Kirkharle, and the Duke of Northumberland's Alnwick.

Few strong geographical patterns emerge. A few firm groups appear, such as Brown's early Warwickshire commissions in the 1740s–50s, from the family and social networks of the country-house owners, and their connections with the gentleman architect Sanderson Miller. At this time the two men were linked in various ways. As many of Brown's early commissions were connected with Miller or his group of landed friends, Miller was probably recommending him as a bright prospect.

Aristocratic word-of-mouth recommendation as well as patronage was essential for Brown's topnotch career to prosper. Lord Cobham's influence remained great, even after his death in 1749, and Brown's early group of patrons in the 1740s and early 1750s were also linked socially and politically with his old employer. The Stowe, Petworth and Warwickshire connections are typical of this complex and confusing web. For the 5th Earl of Desmond at Newnham Paddox in 1746 the formal 'great canal' was altered 'by a Plan and the direction of Mr Brown, Gardiner to Lord Cobham' on Cobham's recommendation; here Brown supervised work in the grounds until *c*.1770. At nearby Warwick Castle he completed the removal of the formal gardens for Lord Brooke in 1749 and remodelled the park in the 1750s–60s. From 1748 plans were in preparation for Packington, where there was a family connection with Lord Egremont. The recommendation of Brown to Lord Egremont for Petworth probably came via his relations including his brother-in-law at Wotton, and Packington. In turn Lord Egremont seems to have recommended Brown to Lord Anson in 1753 to lay out Moor Park, Hertfordshire, and possibly at Holkham, begun in 1762 for the widow of the Earl of Leicester.

The king: the highest in the land

Not until the middle of Brown's career, in 1764, did serious royal patronage come his way, when he was appointed 'Master Gardener' at royal Hampton Court and 'Gardener' at St James's (see page 38).

As soon as he took up his royal post he started making great alterations to the 25-year-old George III's Richmond Gardens. This is now the western half of Kew Gardens alongside the Thames opposite Syon, which itself was about to get a further make-over from Brown from 1767 to 1773 after his initial work in the mid-1750s. The young king, who had an interest in architecture fostered by the Earl of Bute, took a great interest in the alterations and had an easy relationship with Brown. The king's mother, Princess Augusta, had developed the adjacent eastern estate (now the east half of Kew Gardens) alongside the Kew Road and brought in Brown's main rival William Chambers to improve her grounds. Brown provided three versions of the one plan that survives, but the layout was altered from this.

With his royal post Brown found exceptional access to George III, and to his rather unpredictable ear. Clearly the king would at least listen to what Brown had to say and the Royal Gardener was wise enough not to push things too far. On occasion he acted as intermediary between Pitt the Elder and the king, for in 1777 he reported to Pitt that he had been 'heard with attention' by His Majesty on the ticklish matter of American hostilities. His diplomacy was suitably nuanced for as he put it 'I went as far as I durst' on the matter 'upon such tender ground'. Later in the year he continued to have many opportunities for 'favourable conversations' with the King, in which 'no acrimony, nor ill will appeared'.

He also drew up plans for the grounds of Buckingham Palace, apparently not executed, but at heart George III did not really understand him and other royals avoided him.

BELOW | At Kew, Brown and William Chambers worked on adjacent parks for the King and his mother, Princess Augusta, respectively. Brown's scheme for Richmond Gardens (top of plan) is distinct from Chambers' style for Kew Gardens (bottom of plan) (*Plan of the Royal Manor of Richmond*, Peter Burrell/ Thomas Richardson, 1771).

Six prime ministers – an unbeatable client list

Brown's list of six prime ministers as clients and their eight parks is unbeatable. While in the throes of complex political machinations, and sometimes while running the country, these men found the time and energy to commission Brown and take an active interest in his work on their estates. They numbered the 4th Duke of Devonshire (PM 1756–7) at Chatsworth around 1760; the 3rd Earl of Bute (PM 1762–3) at Luton Hoo, 1760s–82, and Highcliffe, c.1775; the Rt Hon. George Grenville (PM 1763–5) at Wotton Underwood, 1750s; William Pitt 'the Elder', 1st Earl of Chatham (PM 1766–8) at Burton Pynsent, 1765; the 3rd Duke of Grafton (PM 1768–70) at Euston Suffolk, 1767–69; and the 2nd Earl of Shelburne (PM 1782–3) at Bowood, Wiltshire and Wycombe Abbey, Buckinghamshire, c.1757–62. All were Whigs, except for the Tory Bute. Most of their fellow cabinet ministers were also busy laying out estates in the only patriotic style there was, the English landscape garden, and many employed Brown.

He served another Prime Minster, Lord North (PM 1770–82), whose seat at Wroxton, Oxfordshire, he never got his hands on. On one occasion North sent a letter from Downing Street asking for fruit from Hampton Court to serve a deputation from Oxford University for dinner. Presumably he wanted an exotic selection to dazzle the dons with. Perhaps Brown sent him the most prized of all fruit, pineapples.

While Brown professed no public political allegiance he was a Whig follower. This was not surprising as his greatest patrons were mostly Whigs. However, his sound business sense overrode his political inclinations and allowed him to straddle the political divide so that he had several prominent Tories as clients. These included Lord Bute (Luton Hoo, Highcliffe and his son's Cardiff Castle) and at the end of his career, Thomas Harley at Berrington Hall, near Leominster in Herefordshire.

Pitt the Elder – another man of genius

As important as his friendship with Lord Coventry was, Brown had a strong and similarly enduring connection with the greatest Whig statesman of his age, Pitt the Elder, until his death in 1778. Although Prime Minister for only two years (1766–8), before this he effectively served in this role in all but name throughout the premierships of the Dukes of Newcastle and Devonshire, engineering the genesis of the British Empire. Conquering India, Canada, the West Indies and West Africa were all immensely beneficial to Britain's merchants, although the government was nearly bankrupted.

Pitt the Elder's complex web of family, social and political connections were to bring Brown many commissions including Petworth, Wotton Underwood and Broadlands. William Pitt began as one of the political circle of younger men patronised by Whig Lord Cobham while in the political wilderness of his later years, known as Cobham's Cubs, so he knew Stowe well from the 1730s and Brown in the 1740s, and became a great admirer.

Pitt's connection with Wotton and Stowe was cemented by a whirlwind romance when in September 1754, he fell in love with Lady Hester Grenville, daughter of Richard Grenville of Wotton Hall, and Hester Grenville, Countess Temple. Pitt knew her from her girlhood as sister to his fellow Cubs Richard Grenville (now Earl Temple) and George and James. In October, the couple were engaged; the wedding took place on 16 November 1754, 'the day from which I shall date all the real honour and happiness of poor life'. Brown was

ABOVE | Pitt the Elder, one of the six prime ministers Brown worked for. He also advised two Earls of Bristol at Ickworth, Suffolk, including the 4th Earl (here with his son). The Georgian political elite was obsessed with architecture and gardening, to Brown's benefit (*John Augustus, later Lord Hervey, being presented by his father to William Pitt the Elder*, William Hoare, 1771).

well acquainted with the Countess, corresponded with her and undertook various personal missions such as looking for a new house for them. In the 1760s Brown worked on their newly acquired park at Burton Pynsent, Somerset. The friendship was well recorded in apocryphal anecdotes, which have the ring of truth. One recounts a chance meeting at Staines when they dined together. As they were about to part Pitt urged Brown 'Go you and adorn England', to which Brown replied 'Go you and preserve it.'

Half the House of Lords

Nobility were more enthusiastic for Brown than royalty. Peers flocked to commission him, at a rough count nearly 80 dukes, marquesses, earls, viscounts, and occasional marchionesses, countesses and other peeresses, not to mention barons and baronets (this last not strictly nobility). The 6th Earl of Coventry, who inherited Croome in 1751 and died in 1809, was foremost among the 'Earls of Creation'. He was also Brown's greatest patron throughout his career after Stowe.

BELOW | Wimpole, Cambridgeshire, was one of Brown's aristocratic commissions, for the Earl of Hardwick in the 1760s.

MPs and the wealthiest men in Britain

In the Other Place MPs were a mixed bag socially and financially but many were keen to employ Brown, particularly the wealthiest in the House of Commons who had a fortune by dint of their own inheritance, native wit or skulduggery and had a country estate that needed Browning.

Some MPs were as wealthy as any Peers, and vied for the title of the richest commoner in England. Needless to say, Brown had many on his books. Of course for much of their friendship career-politician Pitt the Elder was a commoner and MP, and was not created a Baron until in 1776 when the King created him Baron Rivers. Charles Pelham of Brocklesby, in flat and remote Lincolnshire, was a country gentleman with enormous inherited agricultural rents at his disposal. Sir James Lowther of Lowther in even more distant Cumbria inherited the immense wealth of three family members including vast estates in the north-west and plantations in the West Indies. More shadowy was George Durant's sudden wealth. He began as a government clerk in the pay office on £250 a year but after joining the British expedition to Havana as part of the Seven Years' War returned inexplicably wealthy and bought Tong estate in Shropshire, remodelling it extravagantly with Brown's

help. Samuel Whitbread, son of a Bedfordshire yeoman, made his brewery the largest in the country, acquired extensive estates in the county and 'Browned' his estate there at Southill Park.

A wealthy man could ruin himself in three ways it was said: speculation, building and women. MP Sir George Colebrooke managed his own ruination through the first two of these. Brown's work cost him the hefty total of £3,000 as part of the vast sum of £30,000 he spent on his thousand-acre estate at Gatton Park, Surrey, in the 1760s. A leading London merchant and banker, a director and chairman of the East India Company, none of this saved Colebrooke when his rash speculation on raw materials nosedived during a financial crash. By 1777 he was ruined. Ironically although he was MP for Arundel he helped to perpetuate the notorious Rotten Borough of Gatton, which despite returning two MPs had only a handful of voters, who, as the landowner, he controlled. He added the so-called Town Hall in Brown's park in tribute to Gatton's status as a parliamentary borough. A little, elegant open classical roof on columns, it shelters a stone voting urn, where the election results were announced. Luckily Brown was fully paid up before Colebrooke's financial ruin.

BELOW | Sometimes little survives to tell us exactly what Brown did. At Ickworth, he was paid hundreds of pounds but his contribution is unclear. He may have sited the dramatic house in its prominent position.

Merchants, bankers, nabobs

Merchants and bankers used Brown to help them join the ranks of the landed, having recently acquired enough money by dint of commercial acumen. Thomas Harley, the brother of the 4th Earl of Oxford, came from a landed family but took advantage of the Georgian arena to become a sharp banker, government contractor, Lord Mayor of London and MP for Herefordshire. What he needed then was a country seat of suitable taste and splendour. He chose Berrington in Herefordshire, where Brown's son-in-law Holland built the house as the chief garden building in Brown's last great landscape.

Joseph Damer was a typical aspiring newcomer. Recently created Lord Milton and married to the daughter of the first Duke of Dorset, he commissioned Brown to convert a vast area of windswept Dorset downland to a private world of swooping park valleys enclosed by woodland at Milton Abbey in two campaigns in the mid-1760s and 1770s. For his own banker, Robert Drummond, on the Solent at Fawley near Southampton, Brown (with Holland) built a new house set in a park, and devised a pleasure ground walk for a sweet little fishing lodge.

Nabobs were typical of what could be achieved by Georgian entrepreneurship, at a time when fortunes were ripe to be plucked from the Subcontinent by various means. On his return the former Governor of Madras, George Pigot, consulted Brown on his newly acquired Patshull Hall and Old Park. For a mere 50 guineas he got a plan that gave him a spectacular and sinuous lake over a mile long. At Claremont, Surrey, Pigot's sometime deputy Clive of India, having also made his fortune in India, extravagantly commissioned not just a park from Brown but with it a whole new house, paying him £30,000.

The Groves of Academe

The Groves of Academe detained Brown but briefly, after in 1768 he acquired the Lordship of the Manor of Fenstanton only 10 miles from Cambridge. He provided a plan in 1772 to alter the grounds of St John's College straddling the River Cam on The Backs alongside other colleges including King's and Trinity. They took up his scheme to complement major works to the buildings, replacing a group of small walled gardens with a new Wilderness for the Fellows, including a lawn fringed with trees.

Such decisiveness was rare, for the Oxbridge colleges were notorious for commissioning schemes from the great designers and being unable to agree to carry them out. If the members of a single college could seldom agree on change, then when more than one college was involved disagreement was bound to sink the scheme. It happened to Brown when he was asked for a design to unify the five Cambridge college grounds on The Backs between St John's and Queen's. His gently sweeping scheme of 1779 was united by the half-mile long stretch of the Cam broadened into a lazily curving sweep running through parkland. The individuality of the colleges involved triumphed, and Brown's scheme was never executed. For one thing it would have thrown these usually segregated dons together in an unsettlingly random and unpredictable way, let alone the expense and co-operation between colleges involved.

The artistic world also sought his touch. He advised his great friend the actor-playwright and manager Garrick on his villa by the Thames at nearby Hampton. A grottish tunnel was built under the road to link the house with the Temple to Shakespeare on the river bank. On a teeny scale, Frederick Nicolay, Queen Charlotte's trusted talented German music librarian and violinist, sought advice for his modest house in Richmond. He wrote tongue-in-cheek to Brown, saying he was in great Distress and Trouble, over what to do with his large piece of ground (almost half an acre), signing off with, 'I hope it is no offence to wish for a Miniature Picture from a Raphael.'

Beyond England

Beyond England Brown did little directly. In Wales we know of only four commissions, but none were large and all were in his later years. At Newton House (Dinefwr) he made a series of recommendations for the existing landscape park, including the picturesque Brown's Walk, recently partly opened up once more, and designed the kitchen garden as well as an unexecuted Gothic gateway. At Talacre the classical stone banqueting pavilion is very similar to the brick Owl House overlooking the walled garden and park at Wallington. In the Principality there were fewer of the great wealthy families; often they were English or Scottish incomers, absent with their interest taken up by their main estates elsewhere and not inclined to major innovations. It was left to others such as William Emes at Erddig and Chirk, and Adam Mickle at Tredegar to design the grounds for the gentry in lowland Wales for their 'elegant seats' set in parks of 'rich groves and smiling lawns'.

Ireland never welcomed Brown on her soil, but not for lack of interest from prospective clients. The Duke of Leinster was desperate to get him over, offering him £1,000. This being late in his career when he did not need the financial incentive, Brown declined, on the grounds that 'he had not yet finished England'. He did, however, provide designs for alterations to Slane Castle in County Meath and may have designed the park around it (remotely). In Scotland his ex-surveyor Thomas White successfully filled the gap, among others. Although Brown never travelled abroad, he touched both France and Germany. He prepared a plan for 'a French Gentleman' in 1775, and one for an estate intriguingly called Richmond in Braunschweig, Germany in 1767, possibly for Duchess Augusta, sister of George III, for a miniature park or pleasure ground.

And what of the ladies?

In a world in which gentlemen dominated life, the ladies were largely sidelined from formal positions of power and wealth. Men inevitably dominate the roll call of Brown's clients. Even so, in traditional family life wealthy women did influence their husbands. Elizabeth Seymour inherited Syon Park and Alnwick Castle but it is her husband, a keen gardener, that we are told masterminded the great landscaping activities at these places. He did bring in Brown, but as the Northumberlands' marriage was a harmonious and devoted one, it was likely to be a joint decision between husband and wife.

Some ladies were more clearly influential in their dealings with Brown. The young Jemima Grey inherited Wrest Park, Bedfordshire as a Marchioness, a peeress in her own right, in 1740, just before she married Philip Yorke, later Earl of Hardwicke who had Wimpole. She exercised her own ideas about her estate. In 1758 she brought Brown to Wrest, but for a limited purpose. He was not allowed to alter the old-fashioned but dramatic formal core of the Great Garden created by her grandfather. For this she had high regard and was reluctant to make significant alterations. Wrest was, and remains, a magnificent set piece in French style. Instead Brown worked on the periphery of the garden, softening the contours of the outer canals and improving the drainage. Jemima was so enamoured of Brown that she erected a small column as a monument commemorating the works. The inscription reads: 'These gardens originally laid out by Henry Duke of Kent, were altered by Philip Earl of Hardwicke and Jemima Marchioness Grey, with the professional assistance of Lancelot Brown Esq. in the years 1758, 1759, 1760.' She too had a happy and successful marriage, during which Brown was employed on a more innovative scheme on Wimpole.

Occasionally a lady of independent means hired Brown, usually a widow such as Margaret, widow of the Earl of Leicester at Holkham, Norfolk and Lord Cobham's widow at her dower house, Stoke Poges Manor in Bucks. Mrs Elizabeth Montagu, The 'Queen of the Blue Stockings', inhabited a different sphere to these aristocratic ladies. The intellectual and by now mature widow hired Brown in 1781, close to the end of his career, to advise her at Sandleford Priory, near Newbury. Her husband having died and left her a sizeable income, she felt at last able to be creative. Brown cleared the grounds and laid out a simple park and lake (the eponymous Brown's Pond), with views into the hilly Berkshire countryside as the setting for new Gothick rooms by James Wyatt. Here Mrs Montagu, renowned for her intellectual salon, entertained happily and inexhaustibly.

Personal services – how he worked

Brown's work ranged from a single advisory visit for a few guineas, to the creation of a huge layout that required the movement of thousands of tons of earth by hand and a complete remodelling of the grounds at a cost of tens of thousands of pounds. In all these jobs he was the face of the business and his personal attention was key to the service offered. Brown was the person his clients wanted and it was Brown that they got, though sometimes he took a while to get to them.

FIRST VISIT THE SITE AND SURVEY IT

A site visit was essential for a successful result artistically and practically. It is impossible to provide a fully tailored design for a piece of ground without seeing it to gauge its land form, aspect, character and setting. Before planning changes one must know what is present first, even if it is to be altered out of all recognition. Even more so when major engineering works involve water, always a slippery and mercurial element.

BELOW | Some married couples enjoyed planning their grounds together. Philip Yorke, 2nd Earl of Hardwicke, owned Wimpole, Cambridgeshire. His wife Jemima, Marchioness Grey, owned Wrest Park, Bedfordshire. Brown worked for both (Allan Ramsay, 1741).

When a client contacted Brown a date was agreed for him to visit. If he was lucky he could persuade the client to wait until he could fit it in with trips to other jobs. Letters from peers show that they not only had the highest regard for him as a 'Genius whose Taste is so superior and unrivalled', but resorted to flattery, in pleading for a visit, as did Viscount Lisburne when wanting Brown to visit Mamhead in Devon in 1772.

Brown's health also postponed some visits, but this did not deter clients. In August 1773 Lord Arundell of Wardour Castle wrote to Brown that he had long thought about inviting Brown, and had seen several specimens of his 'fine taste', so that he now wanted a general plan for the grounds, water, and so on. Arundell urged Brown to visit when next he was in the neighbourhood for other business, when his lordship would go to the trouble of making himself available to spend some days with him. Brown had still not managed to visit by December and his lordship wrote again, sorry to hear of Brown's indisposition, and still hoping for a visit at some point. Lord Dacre too was patient and solicitous when waiting for Brown to recover from illness.

ABOVE | An idealised pastoral view of Brown's park at Wimpole, Cambridgeshire, where he created a string of lakes across the undulating park (*View of Wimpole Hall, Cambridgeshire, looking South*, Richard Bankes Harraden, 1822).

It is extraordinary that these men of high self-regard, wealth, and in many cases political status, would abase themselves to plead with Brown to proffer his paid services upon them. Lord Abingdon went so far as to say that 'I pay so great Deference to your Taste, Prudence, and Judgment that I never make the least inquiry concerning the improvements' at Rycote, Oxfordshire where he was paying Brown some £3,000 'but shall always be happy to meet you there ... or in any other part of the Globe.'

After a visit, Brown needed the site to be mapped from a ground survey. His two main surveyors were Spyers and Lapidge, who traversed the country following in his widespread footsteps. It was no quick service either. At Tottenham Park Spyers spent three weeks and three days on the survey in 1764. Together the visits and survey were often billed for around £30–£40 (some £4,000–£6,000 today). Surveyors used steel chains and theodolites to map features and distances, triangulating from a fixed base line. It was trickier to measure levels to estimate the earth movement required for lakes. Staking out by trial and error was used and Brown had a particularly good eye for this. A sound grounding in quite complex maths, particularly geometry, was essential to make the calculations accurately together with an understanding of engineering to know what was possible.

Not every job was a winner. As his account book shows, sometimes a job got no further than one or more visits by him and a survey by his man. At Longford Castle, Wiltshire, Brown visited twice, then Spyers surveyed with some levels 'taken carefully', and a year later Brown had to send a letter to Lord Radnor asking for 10 guineas 'for my trouble, etc, etc'. At some places a plan was noted or even more vaguely just a visit or two. At

BELOW | Woodchester Park, Gloucestershire, was one of Brown's final sites, which he visited in 1782. It is in his style, but we know nothing of what he advised or if his advice was carried out.

Boarstall, Buckinghamshire he charged 15 guineas for two visits. At Woodchester, Gloucestershire, he visited in 1782 shortly before his death and Spyers made a survey, but the outcome is unclear, possibly the creation of one extensive lake out of a chain.

The speed of his work was legendary, as one Frenchman noted breathlessly, 'after an hour on horse-back he conceived the design for an entire park, and ... after that, half-a-day was enough for him to mark it out on the ground.'

Next came the planning stage, drawing up a design. Brown must have breathed a sigh of relief when he was left to his own devices without the owner breathing down his neck: as with Lord Abingdon at Rycote, who just wanted the latest fashion around his country house and was content for Brown to use his professional and artistic judgement. In many cases though, the client had seen enough other landscape gardens at the estates of his friends, family and associates, to believe himself qualified to set out ideas of his own. It is impossible in most cases to tell where a design is purely Brown's and where he had to incorporate his client's ideas. We know that the well-informed Lord Coventry had a major role and directed the design at Croome, as did Pitt at Wotton Underwood for the Grenvilles. It is not surprising as these were early projects for Brown. But as his career progressed, how difficult it must have been as an expert to manage clients' expectations and ensure their madder ideas were tempered or gently avoided.

After a site visit Brown returned to Hammersmith, or after 1764 to Wilderness House at Hampton Court. He sent out one of his surveyors to record the current layout, and then drew up a plan or got one of his assistants to do so. At Copped Hall, Essex, where the house is now a glorious, ruined eye-catcher, Brown recorded in his account book: 'For my Journeys and

ABOVE | Brown had sound business sense. His account book, which he kept from 1764 until his death in 1783, tells us who he worked for, where and the sums he charged. 101 clients are recorded in England and Wales.

trouble, etc. for Mr Griffin's admeasurements of the ground round the House £31.10s.0d'. Perhaps he sent a written note of his broad suggestions but a plan is not mentioned and the park did not benefit from his hand, for only over many decades was it encircled by a belt and laid out with pasture and clumps in a very pedestrian design. The glory of the place was and remains the prominent position of the rather stiff classical mansion commanding views of much of south Essex, sadly burnt out in 1917. At Sheffield Park, Sussex, Brown made several journeys, Spyers surveyed in 1776 and one plan, or possibly two were drawn up for 'alterations of the Place particularly for the Water & the Ground about it.'

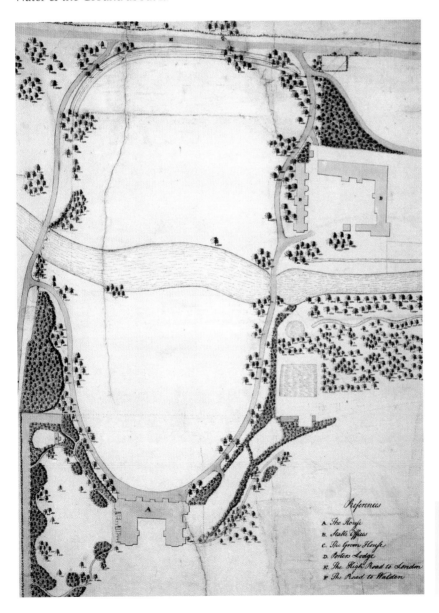

References

A. The House
B. Stable Offices
C. The Green House
D. Porters Lodge
E. The High Road to London
F. The Road to Walden

LEFT | Plans were part of the Brown package. The design for part of Audley End park, Essex, 1763.

THEN SELL THE SCHEME TO THE CLIENT

After the initial visits and survey, if he got as far as a plan Brown would present it to the client. It was always best to present it in person so that the rationale and the artistic vision could be properly explained. For the Earl of Pembroke at Wilton, Spyers made an extensive survey of 'all the Place' covering 1,200 acres for £40, working out at 8d/acre, and for a further £70 a General Plan for the Alterations was made and charged for with Brown's journeys there (obviously more than one). At Byram with only 373 acres the charge was a shilling an acre, with higher travelling expenses. At Basildon Park, in the Berkshire Chilterns, from the nabob Francis Sykes he received 50 guineas 'for my journeys there and for plans of the kitchen garden and stove.'

The difficulties of dealing with prospective clients included those with pretensions to taste who hadn't quite reached the stage of being proper landed owners. A story (perhaps apocryphal) is recounted that Brown was sent for by a gentleman in Staffordshire who had more money than land.

BELOW | The labour involved in creating a landscape park was immense, digging, earth-moving, planting trees, all without mechanical aids. Tredegar, Newport, South Wales, designed by Adam Mickle in a Brownian style.

Brown cast his eye over the land shown to him. His advice was typical: 'That hill you must clump.' But the reply was 'That I cannot do for it belongs to Mr Jennings.' So Brown tried again, 'Well, – we must pass over that; this valley must be cleared and floated.' Again difficulties: 'Impossible, returned the other, for that is also Mr Jennings's.' At this point our hero lost patience: 'Your most humble servant, said Brown, taking an abrupt leave, I think Mr Jennings should have sent for me not you' (*Morning Post*, 30 July 1774).

Where the outcome was more assured, he was happy to stick to his guns, playing off his clients' parsimony against their aspirations to fashion. Even his best clients sometimes needed a bit of gentle persuasion, appealing to their innate good taste. At Burghley Lord Exeter asked him how much the cost for floating the lake would be, as the nearby house flooded and drainage was vital. Brown, it is said, replied rather coyly, 'The Goddess of Taste will reproach you, My Lord, if you think of expence in so divine a place.' Still his lordship hesitated. Brown put his foot down and refused to budge. 'It will take several years to do it, I must have two thousand a year for it till it is done'. Needless to say, he got the job on those terms and was employed there from 1756 for many years.

WHAT DID YOU GET FOR £100?

For £100 or sometimes 100 guineas (equivalent to some £10,000–£12,000 today) the client could obtain a visit, a survey by one of Brown's assistants and a design plan (as at Lleweni, Denbighshire, 1782). This took about six months. Then if the client wished, it was up to him to put the design on the ground, usually a winter job, sometimes over several seasons. The working drawings were usually used to destruction, but presentation plans were works of art in their own right, items of prestige, often displayed in the estate office. The payment of a round sum suggests that the fee was for advice and perhaps a survey and a plan, rather than an itemised sum for labour. Brown seldom supplied plants, leaving the client to deal with nurserymen.

A plan was produced by an assistant of Brown (probably Lapidge) for Hatfield Forest, the dead flat detached pleasure ground to Jacob Houblon's Hallingbury Place, Essex. Jacob, from a family of merchant-princes of London, paid Brown £100 in 1758. The scheme modified the recently built 11-acre lake, softening its rather crude lines into sinuous wavy banks; a 'river' at either end carried the inlet and outlet channels of the stream, each with its own tiny island to disguise the ends of the water. This provided a fashionable setting for the dear little Shell House, an elegant tea house, the only garden building overlooking the lake in the ancient oak forest. In the cottage behind a good woman kept Mrs Houblon's poultry and peacocks, considered very

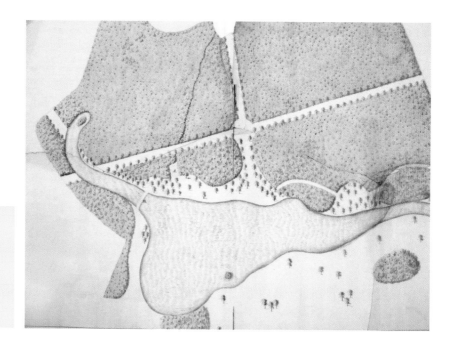

RIGHT | For Hatfield
Forest, Essex, Brown's
1757 presentation plan, is a
conveniently sized 60 x 90cm
(2 x 3ft). His suggestions were
only partly carried out.

good eating. As quite often happened, only portions of Brown's scheme
were taken on board. The harshly straight dam that Brown hoped to soften
into a sensuous curve remained, presumably because his proposal was too
expensive, and only one of the 'rivers' was created, along the outlet.

Ralph Allen of Prior Park was charged £100, presumably for the preliminary
package of visits by Brown, a survey by his man, and a design plan softening
the earlier landscape. He may also have advised on the huge Palladian Bridge,
which looks as though it has crash landed across the bottom of the steep
valley overlooking Bath, below the enormously wide house, which was the
marketing tool for the man who made his money out of supplying the Bath
stone to build the city.

At Newton House (Dinefwr Castle), in hilly and remote south-west Wales,
Brown visited, then sent suggestions for disparate parts within the grounds,
which had already been landscaped in the modern style. Clearly impressed,
he wrote to his client George Rice, 'I wish my journey may prove of use to
the place, which if it should, it will be very flattering to me. Nature has been
truly bountiful and art has done no harm'. 'Mr Brown's Directions', dated
1776, included moving the kitchen garden to the edge of the park, laying out
a mile-long circuit walk from the house around the park, moving the park
entrance and building a Gothic gateway for the new entrance (which was
ignored). His account book details journeys, plans for the kitchen garden
and walls and a design for the new gateway.

ABOVE | The view over the
Palladian Bridge at Prior Park
Landscape Garden uses the city
of Bath and surrounding hills as
part of the scene.

Sometimes the owner was tempted to take credit for Brown's design, as at
Kings Weston in Bristol and probably Tong Castle. In other cases, such as
Lowther in Cumbria, despite visits and one or more plans supplied it seems
that his advice was not taken up at all.

DRAWING UP THE SCHEME

The plans were generally ink and watercolour, showing items to be removed,
such as the rigid line of the dam at Hatfield Forest, lightly dotted in on the
1757 plan. Brown also used this notation on his *c*.1770 plan for Kirkharle,
his home village estate, in which he dotted in the outlines of the old formal
gardens, buildings and other features specifying they were 'to be taken away'.
The plan is in ink, pencil and brown wash. Kirkharle plan shows three types
of tree: deciduous, conifer, and weeping, each with its shadow; horizontal
brush strokes represent water in which trees are reflected with vigorous
staccato treatment of the expanses of woodland. Typical of his design features
were clumps of trees, encircling belts, a serpentine river created from a stream
(but not executed) and a serpentine drive.

Plan sizes varied. For the largest sites his park plans filled a wall, as for the 1,200-acre Bowood (1763). The 1752 plan for 650-acre Petworth Park is around 152 x 90cm (5 x 3ft) and is the only survivor of several plans he delivered. Perhaps this plan survives because it was never used, but was superseded by a later design. The second plan produced for Heveningham, Suffolk, is another monster at some 3m (10ft) across (1782), for it extends over the further parts of the grounds and includes a long sinuous river proposal. Other plans were more modest. The presentation plan for Hatfield Forest is just 60 x 90cm (2 x 3ft). Lowther Park plans measured around 91 x 183cm (3 x 6ft), and the unexecuted plan for the Cambridge Backs measured some 152 x 76cm

BELOW | Country gentlemen of taste employed Brown, such as Sir Walter Calverley Blackett in Northumberland at Wallington and Rothley Lakes in the 1760s (Joshua Reynolds, c.1762).

(5 x 2½ft). The working plan for Ashburnham Place, Sussex is just over 1.2 x 2m (4 x 6½ft), while the accompanying building plans and elevations are more conveniently sized. These sorts of plans and elevations for details such as bridges, particular areas of the grounds and garden buildings were usually of this scale. At Rothley Lower Lake his head of the water plan and an elevation of a sham rustic arched bridge each measured about 30 x 46cm (1 x 1½ft).

THE PLAN ON THE GROUND

After the plan was agreed Brown was flexible about how it was put on the ground. He might remain involved in two main ways. Sometimes he offered advice on the execution to the owner's men carrying out the work. This probably happened at Lacock Abbey, Wiltshire, where £200 was charged but there are no firm details of what this sum was for.

A foreman hired the labourers and directed operations, or else estate labour was used. Brown popped in

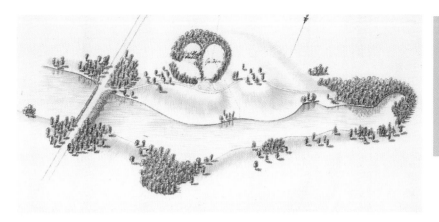

occasionally to check progress, ensure that all was going well and the client was happy. Even in the early 1750s he had four foremen working for him on various jobs and during his career he employed over 20. Labourers were paid by the foremen several shillings a day for six days a week, less for old men, boys and women, but probably with lodging and fuel provided. Many of his major designs were supervised in this way, including Chatsworth, Burghley and Alnwick. He probably supervised the estate staff in this way at Ickworth. From 1769–73, four payments were made of between £150 and £250 totalling £781, plus considerable sums to Henry Holland, presumably for Ickworth Lodge, the Hervey family's long-term 'temporary' home before the great rotunda was begun. These sums are probably for supervisory work of the Earl of Bristol's men, say £200 per winter season. The mess and disruption must have been considerable.

The advice and supervision was adapted to suit the circumstances. At Alnwick between 1750 and 1786, a landscape park was developed for the 1st Duke of Northumberland, with the supervision of work by Brown and his foremen Cornelius Griffin, Robson and Biesley in the 1760–80s, working alongside James and Thomas Call, the Duke's gardeners. Brown's foremen worked with teams of men between 1771 and 1781 and records show that they also worked alongside Call and his men (in 1773 for example, Brown's Biesley had a team of 78 and the Duke's Call a team of 60).

COSTS OF PUTTING THE PLAN ON THE GROUND

The more lucrative practice, and the way to ensure that things went exactly as Brown planned, was to carry out the work on the ground with his own men. At Petworth, a project first mooted while he was still at Stowe, he had another opportunity early in his career to work for one of the wealthiest of men, the 2nd Earl of Egremont, who had recently become one of the richest peers in England and a phenomenon (and brother-in-law of George Grenville of Wotton Underwood, sister landscape to Stowe). Brown transformed the park at Petworth. Away went the outdated formal gardens and walled enclosures, rather as he did later at Blenheim. In came ha-has, lakes and sweeping carriage drives with spectacular views of surrounding Sussex. This was not isolated from others of Lord Egremont's projects. It was an integral part of the Earl's vision, executed in a massive 13-year spending spree from 1750 in which he refurnished the house, and collected priceless pictures and antique sculpture,

which he housed in a new purpose-built gallery. He spent prodigious sums on employing Brown to make similarly spectacular changes to the gardens and park. The 1752 plan is fascinatingly supplemented by contracts worth £5,500 (some £500,000 today) between 1753 and 1765 for the various main works, detailing the tasks to be undertaken, and bills from nurseryman John Williamson including trees, flowering shrubs and evergreens. Brown's suggestions on the surviving plan were largely implemented for the park, but to a lesser extent for the pleasure ground.

At his last major set piece, Berrington Hall, Herefordshire, after a survey by Lapidge and a 'plan of alterations' (which does not survive), four payments

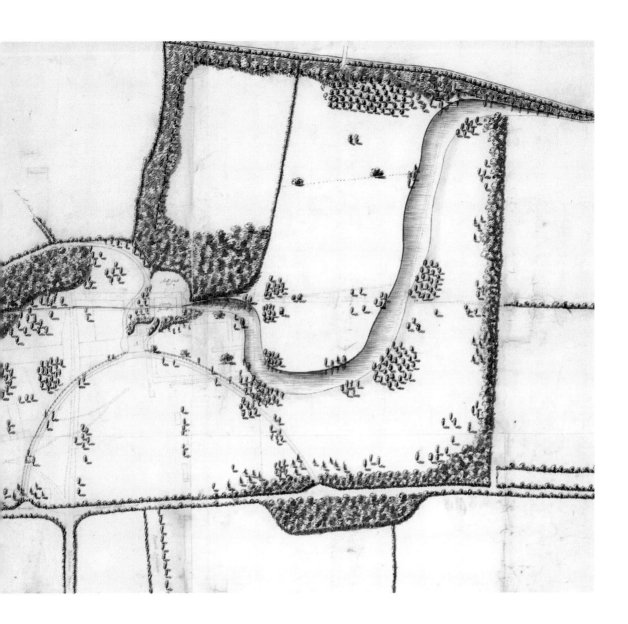

totalling £1,600 (£170,000 today) resulted in a fine landscape that after his death in 1783 continued to be laid out according to his vision.

At Ashridge nearly £3,000 is recorded in the account book as paid by the 'Canal Duke' of Bridgewater between 1762 and 1768. It was perhaps mostly for Holland's building works on the new house (now the site of the Wyatville Orangery), but partly for laying out the dry Chiltern Golden Valley, which is very similar in its secluded Arcadian character to the Grecian Valley at Stowe but without buildings and sculpture. He also seems to have provided a pleasure ground behind Holland's new house with island beds set in lawns,

breaking up the old formal yew-lined parterre and keeping the yews for structure. In Surrey Sir George Colebrooke was paying a sequence of similar sums for another extensive commission at Gatton Park, totalling £3,055, excluding later journeys and a plan of the Great Water and Menagerie.

Wimpole was a landscape commission on a similar financial scale, a very watery one, with a string of lakes and the construction of Sanderson Miller's picturesque Gothic ruin as the park eye-catcher (this design had hung around unbuilt for some years). For this he was paid £3,400, with £200–£300 every few months between 1767 and 1772, when the tower was still being put up. Lord Hardwicke, writing on Christmas Eve 1767, urged Brown to draw up the schedule of forthcoming works and expenses for the following years so that the plan would be complete by 1770. His client was prudent, 'Perhaps it is absurd to look so far forward but however the sketch of the whole may be of use in every event', adding a seasonal postscript that 'If it were not too old-fashioned I wd make you the Complimts of the season'.

Still more extensive, Harewood and Moor Park cost in the region of £6,000 to £7,000, getting on for half a million pounds today. At Ashburnham Place, we have not only Brown's account book, recording a steady payment of several hundred pounds every year by the Earl of Ashburnham from 1767 to 1781, but also his plan of proposals for the layout in his own hand and drawings for a group of buildings. He was paid over £10,000 by Lord Bute for Luton Hoo during the decade to 1774, as well as considerable sums for the Earl's London house in the 1770s, and a further £900 for Luton Hoo and Highcliffe Castle, Dorset, in 1778–9.

A few stratospheric sums catch the eye in his account books. Lord Palmerston at Broadlands paid £21,150 (roughly equivalent to £1.5 million) from 1766–78, for remodelling the house in local white brick with a fine stone portico and laying out the park around it. Clive of India paid £30,000 (around £2m today), from 1769 to 1774, largely for the house but also for remodelling the park. The rewards for an acute nabob were vast and trickled down to his employees, but Clive did not enjoy his magnificent new home for long as he took his own life in November 1774. Still more extraordinary was the sum spent at Blenheim. After a very modest 55-guinea survey of the 2,314 acres at Blenheim and a complex survey plan by Spyers, around £21,500 was received over ten years from 1763 to 1774 by Brown for works just to the park layout and several park buildings, without touching Vanbrugh's house.

Croome – A three-decade masterwork

Croome, begun *c.*1751, was perhaps the most important single commission of Brown's career. A newspaper in 1774 noted that having carried out much work there Brown 'esteems it his best performance'. It was certainly his showcase. Not only did it take him from the very beginning as a freelancer to the literal end (remember Brown died after dining with Lord Coventry, the 6th Earl) but, as his patron, Lord Coventry was influential and championed him. Croome could be criticised as not of the most outstanding quality of design, but it is huge and complex and was lavishly ornamented.

Eventually the job covered 1,000 acres, including garden buildings, the rebuilding of the house and new stables, all as a great set-piece design. The initial draining of the morass and laying out of the grounds at the beginning of Brown's career for Lord Coventry was a major part of the first intensive phase of landscape work, 1751–6, when the greatest transformation occurred. As part of it the mansion, the nursery wing, and the first stage of the office and stable court were built (possibly with advice from Sanderson Miller); four major shrubberies were laid out on earthwork terraces; the Rotunda was built; the park was expanded to the south and east; the artificial river was lengthened; the extensive area of park and the fields were drained; belts were planted, and the church was started to Brown's design (later completed internally by Robert Adam). The lake may have been laid out then or in the early 1760s.

The second phase, for which payments are recorded, seems to relate to Croome, but the Earl did have properties elsewhere. Between 1760 and 1765 around £4,000 was billed. The mansion interiors were completed; there was further work on the belts, shrubberies and park planting; the park was expanded further; Dunstall Castle was built as an eyecatcher from the house and the lake pleasure grounds were established with Brown's grotto, wooden bridges and the Dry Arch Bridge carrying the main drive. Various grand garden buildings were built by Adam including a greenhouse in the pleasure ground.

The landscape at Croome in the 1750s and 1760s was typical of Brown's work, but what we see is probably as much Lord Coventry's vision as Brown's, if not more so. Stylistically it is similar to Burghley (1754 onwards), Syon (mid-1750s and 1767–73), Petworth (1752–63) and especially Packington (*c.*1750). Similar features to those at Croome were used in these, and other, landscapes, such as the house at Newnham Paddox, the grottoes at Clandon, Packington and Rothley (Sham Bridge), the rock arches at Claremont and Wardour, and the menageries at Petworth, Castle Ashby and Gatton Park.

Brown's enduring and affectionate friendship with many clients is epitomised by Croome. At one point, in late 1772, when poor Lord Coventry's river had started to leak he asked for Brown's help. Would Brown please send his own direction to fix the problem, together with 'a Man of Practice', preferably Mr Read, the foreman who had done the work originally? Lord Coventry added pathetically that his enjoyment of Croome the next summer depended on it. Despite this potential difficulty he still invited Brown 'heartily' to a 'Christmas Gambol' and signed himself, as usual, 'your sincere friend'.

ABOVE | It was said of Brown that 'so clearly did he copy nature that his works will be mistaken for it'. At Croome, Worcestershire, it is hard to believe that Brown's mile-long 'river' draining the park is artificial, fed by great masonry culverts.

CHAPTER 3

The omnipotent magician – the secret of Brown's success

Lo! He Comes,
The omnipotent magician, Brown appears.
… He speaks. The lake in front becomes a lawn,
Woods vanish, hills subside, and valleys rise,
And streams, as if created for his use,
Pursue the track of his directing wand.

WM Cowper, *The Task*, Bk III, 1785

The genius of Brown and the place

Brown's creations are magical. Not for nothing was he called the omnipotent magician as he conjured up divine pastoral landscapes from unpromising sites – anything from a windswept barren downland to a soggy morass. Yes, he worked to a formula. Trees, grass and water were his simple ingredients to create the English Landscape Garden. His gift was in tailoring them to the 'genius of the place', the *genius loci*, the unique conditions and form of the site, and its views and setting, to make something that looked beautiful yet felt entirely natural and soothing. As one visitor described '[it] has the most sublime effect... The harmony of the whole diffuses a congenial calm over the imagination and whilst we gaze with rapture, every passion subsides into a most pleasing serenity.'

It is easy to read the design of a Brown landscape once you know what to look for. This chapter explains the elements that he used – simple palette of features was endlessly versatile when expertly and artistically applied to the uniqueness of a particular place: water as lake or river, sweeping grass in a park broken up by clumps and single trees, pleasure grounds and flower gardens, a kitchen garden, usually surrounded by woodland and belts. Some of his plans seem simple and possibly even boring until you see them in the reality of the site and marvel at the effects he could create, apparently effortlessly, with trees, grass and water on a huge scale.

He needed a strong three-dimensional image of the site in his mind to be able to work out how to make the most of its 'genius': how to shelter it, lay out drives to the house, and to screen and frame the views. Parks were meant to look like pictures. To achieve this he used clumps of trees of various shapes and sizes to control the views, blocking some and framing others. Sometimes a single tree divides the view purposely or is put in the only place where it does not block views. In this way he created a complex mesh of view lines within and beyond the setting that are often not fully obvious today. Distant church towers, ancient ruins and hills were favourite targets, subtly framed with foreground trees.

Brown designed relatively few great set pieces from scratch – Croome early in his career and Berrington at the end are classics. At Croome he removed existing gardens and laid out a 1,000-acre park. At Berrington he worked with his son-in-law, architect Henry Holland, on a blank canvas to produce a whole 400-acre scene, house and all. More often he incorporated and modified earlier layouts. At Petworth, another early masterpiece, the previous vestiges were so well integrated that the 650-acre park seems of a piece.

PREVIOUS PAGE | Berrington Hall across the lake, created as part of `Capability' Brown's last great scheme in the 1780s.

LEFT | View from the steps of the house at Berrington Hall, Herefordshire, towards Wales.

Brown's plan shows how well he made use of the existing layout, adapting rather than removing features: he put two ponds where there was already water; he shaped a triangular clump of elms by the larger lake rather than fell it; and he kept a row of chestnuts along the edge of the pleasure ground and other main chestnut groves.

At Blenheim Palace he did this to such effect that it is now a UNESCO World Heritage Site, in large part because of his artistry, and it is regarded as his masterwork. Even the king, when he saw the 2,500 acres of Blenheim, was moved to say 'We have nothing equal to this'.

Often Brown worked on a particular part of a park, such as the gardens and Golden Valley at Ashridge, the lake at Hatfield Forest, the kitchen garden and Brown's Walk at Newton Park (Dinefwr), and the walled garden at Basildon Park. He could also turn his hand to commissions on a relatively small scale. The pleasure ground he laid out at Boarn Hill Cottage, Cadland in Hampshire, for Holland's thatched *cottage orné* fishing lodge, is only 15 acres. This exquisite landscape park in miniature used glimpsed views of the Solent and its shipping to great effect.

Sometimes Brown escaped the park altogether – the ride through the Stag Park in the outer reaches of the Petworth Estate leads to his Deer Park. He devised rides around Wallington Estate, and forest rides at Tottenham and Hatfield. Where arable land was required to be kept but beautified he threw woodland around it. At Petworth he did this with farmland areas on either side of the park. One drive entered across the deep farmed valley at the elegant Gohanna Lodges, named after one of the Earl's racehorses, eye-catching in the distance from the pleasure ground.

A master of his style – the English Landscape Garden

Brown made himself a master of the style that Lord Cobham, William Kent and company pioneered in the 1730s and 1740s, and Brown then added his artistic genius and personal panache. He was not the originator nor the only one doing it, but he became the 'face' of that style. While he was learning at Stowe in the 1740s others were launching the concept elsewhere. Kent's late designs, such as Euston in Suffolk, created scenes at a parkland scale. In Sanderson Miller's designs at places like Farnborough or Alscot in Warwickshire, lakes adorned the middle distance, belts of forest trees enclosed the park, clumps were dotted around the pasture and, more prosaically, much effort was given to drainage.

Brown took these principles further, eventually placing more emphasis on the effects from planting and less on ornamental buildings, which also helped to reduce the cost.

His 'informal' planting echoed Claude Lorrain's idealised paintings of Italian scenery that the Grand Tourists wanted to evoke at home: the sense of calm, an expansive sky and golden light on temples and ruins of classical buildings, all contained in an idyllic wooded and pastoral setting. This was what he and his like were aiming for in the estates of the British *milordi*: the countryside of Italy. Brown developed the intricate pleasure-ground idea of Chiswick and the Elysian Fields at Stowe into a more practical park and estate setting.

The ha-ha – a sunken wall around the pleasure ground that formed a boundary without interrupting the view – became his trademark, which he used to such great effect to unlock his design palette and deceive the eye of the beholder into seeing a limitless park. This had already been tried and tested for several decades and he used it to evoke a sense of liberty and uplifting beauty.

Pearls from the Master's lips setting out his style are tantalising and only partially illuminating. He wrote only one detailed paragraph about his intentions as a designer, in 1775, explaining a design he was sending to a French client. 'Gardening and Place-Making', he wrote, 'when rightly understood will supply all the elegance and all the comforts which Mankind wants in the Country and (I will add) if right, be exactly fit for the owner, the Poet and the Painter.'

To produce these effects Brown set out a list of essential ingredients:

- A good plan
- Good execution
- A perfect knowledge of the country and the objects in it, whether natural or artificial
- Infinite delicacy in the planting etc.
- So much Beauty depending on the size of the trees and the colour of their leaves to produce the effect of light and shade so very essential to the perfecting of a good plan
- Hiding what is disagreeable
- Shewing what is beautiful
- Shade from the large trees
- Sweets [scent] from the smaller sorts of shrubs etc.

Still more vaguely in 1782 he described his style in grammatical terms: '"Now there" said he, pointing his finger, "I make a comma, and there" pointing to another spot, "where a more decided turn is proper, I make a colon; at another part, where an interruption is desirable to break the view, a parenthesis; now a full stop, and then I begin another subject".'

These words are frustratingly brief and in a sense state the perfectly obvious. But they are the best we have. The rest we have to glean second-hand from analysing his plans, accounts of what others thought he was doing, paintings and sketches, and what still remains out in his parks.

Brown never forgot the importance of the bond between land and landscape. Stowe, the most influential of the landscaped gardens then in the making, was the ideal training place for an ambitious young man aspiring to become

BELOW | Magnificent view of the west front of Petworth House, West Sussex, seen over the lake.

a 'place-maker'. Croome was one of his largest place-making undertakings involving land reclamation and building work. Early on he learnt to ride or walk all round the estate to get a good feel for the lie of the land, marking out rides for viewpoints and noting where convex and concave slopes could be exposed or made, and sheets of water floated: 'hideing what is disagreeable and shewing what is beautiful'. This he did with famous speed and flair.

Part of Brown's genius was in putting water in its proper place – away from the house, and relegated to the middle distance in views from the windows – but this was not unique to him. Some competitors were equally adept, such as Adam Mickle at Tredegar in the 1780s.

Formality was not entirely wiped away in many sites. From the 1720s walls, clipped hedges and topiary began to be removed and lines softened and simplified. By the 1750s owners of the walled, formal gardens of an earlier era were finding them very outdated. Some clients, however, having employed Brown for his modern style, may have insisted on keeping much-loved established landscape features, not least because many avenues and other formal plantings were barely mature. Geometric features were adeptly incorporated if necessary. Mainly these plantings were avenues or, in a compromise, he broke them into clumps. Writers continued to recommend planting avenues and many avenues survived. The mesh of avenues at Moor Park, Hertfordshire, survived long after Brown had landscaped the grounds, as did Bridgeman's vast avenues at Wimpole. The great stepped cascade at Chatsworth survived, and occasionally parterres too, such as at Wotton Underwood, along with the great formal enclosed forecourt and avenues.

Mature park trees from an earlier park established an instant patina of age. The fine beeches at Luton Hoo formed the basis for Brown's design, while he greatly extended the 150-year-old park. The magnificent sweet chestnuts at Burghley, planted by Queen Elizabeth's right-hand man William Cecil from the 1550s, were cherished within later schemes.

Sometimes Brown modified only part of the estate. At Wrest Park he was not allowed to make major changes to the formal pleasure ground, which Horace Walpole described as 'very ugly in the old fashioned manner with high hedges and canals'. We must be thankful that Brown was not asked to remove this *tour de force* of Versailles-type landscaping.

Diverse ornaments: garden buildings and sculpture

Brown's buildings will be dealt with more fully in the next chapter. They played a key role as landscape design features, as ornaments essential to punctuate and enliven his designs. In his schemes not all buildings by any means were designed by him. He often worked alongside other architects, from the nationally known Adam, Chambers and Wyatt, to local men such as Hiorns in the Midlands.

Buildings were used in different quantities, and had all sorts of looks and uses. The country house itself was usually the most important building in the landscape design, forming its focus. It was sometimes on a plateau, such as Berrington, or at the break of a slope, or sometimes part-way down a slope, such as Claremont, which stands on its own little rise. Croome Court stands

LEFT | The Lakeside urn designed by Robert Adam at Croome, Worcestershire.

in the bottom of the valley but the landscape most of the way around it is open and never far from the viewer's eye. Ideally the house was sheltered behind, and open to views on at least three sides to and from the main public rooms. The garden front overlooked main views and usually had a garden door to the pleasure ground or even the park (Petworth). Five vistas converge on the garden front at Wotton, some framed by avenues and usually terminating at sculptures.

The classical portico made a great viewing platform. This is a roof supported by open columns, often above a grand sweeping staircase leading to the front door. As a glorified porch it provided an elevated outdoor viewpoint conveniently protected from rain and bright sunshine. The columns framed set views as epitomised at Croome, Claremont and Berrington.

In most cases Brown designed a park around an existing house, which he may have remodelled. Occasionally, as at Ickworth, there was no house at all, for the old manor house had by the time Brown arrived been demolished with the intention to build another one in a quite different spot overlooking the main park valley. Presumably he had to work around the projected site of the new building, which he never saw built in its stunning drum-like form with great wings.

Historians are divided as to whether he used fewer buildings as his career progressed, but really all we can say is that some of his designs have fewer buildings than others. An abundance of garden and park buildings populate his early commissions at Wotton Underwood and Croome (both 1750s). Just as often, there were next to none, regardless of when he designed during his career. This is so for his early Petworth (1750s), Ashridge's Golden Valley (1760s), and his last great work, Berrington (c.1781). At Wotton Underwood the plethora of buildings (essential to the landscape experience as each is a viewpoint for several views), were largely of ephemeral timber, possibly specified by Pitt the Elder.

This contrasted with the magnificent stone park and garden edifices at Stowe, and at Croome where no expense was spared. Few buildings were put up by him at the contemporary Petworth. A classical temple stands in the pleasure ground and a hefty stone boathouse by the lake (notwithstanding various lodges and the rotunda put up after his time), and he was said not to be in favour of an excess of buildings there. He used the elegant little 1740s Shell House at Hatfield Forest as the focus of the detached pleasure ground around which his design of 1757 pivoted.

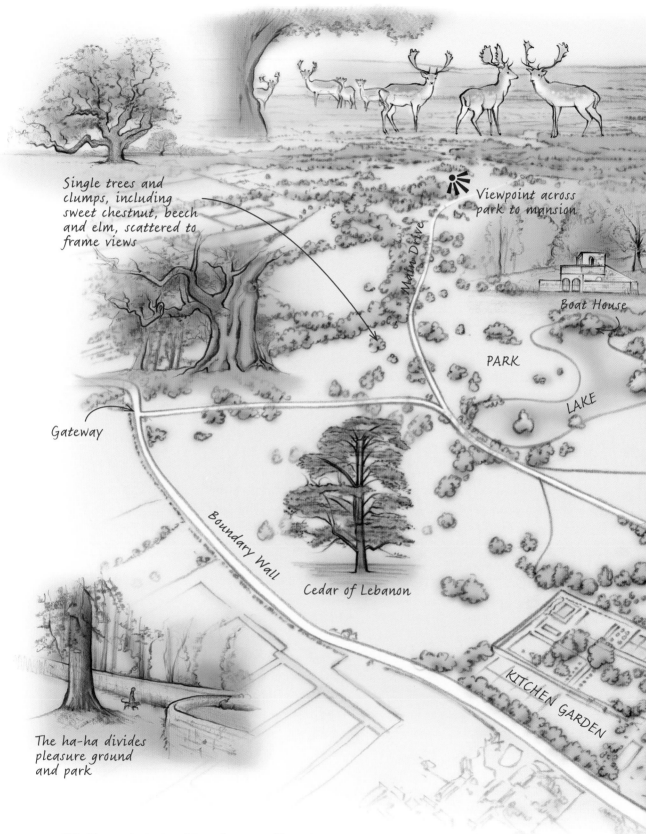

Single trees and clumps, including sweet chestnut, beech and elm, scattered to frame views

Viewpoint across park to mansion

Main Drive

Boat House

PARK

LAKE

Gateway

Boundary Wall

Cedar of Lebanon

KITCHEN GARDEN

The ha-ha divides pleasure ground and park

Brown's design palette

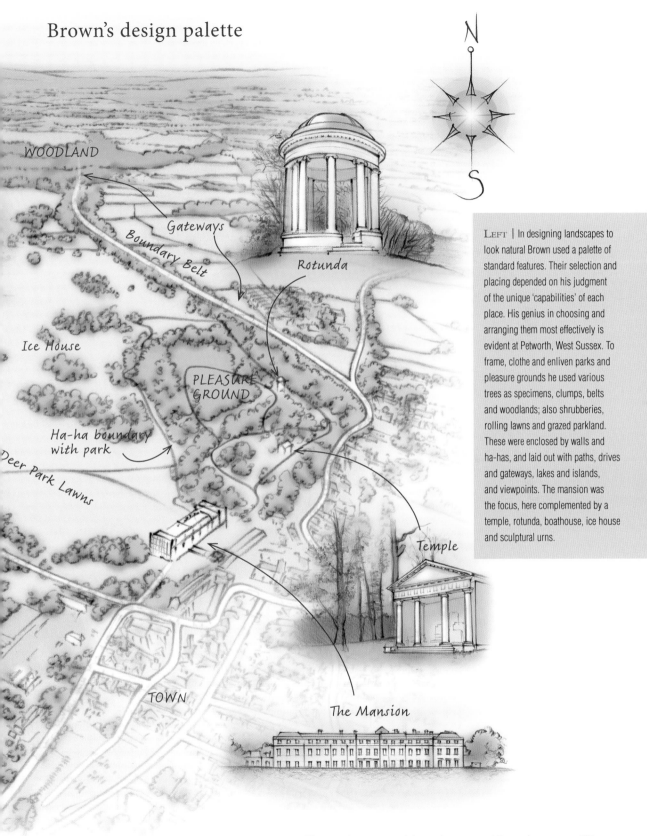

N

S

WOODLAND

Gateways

Boundary Belt

Rotunda

Ice House

PLEASURE GROUND

Ha-ha boundary with park

Deer Park Lawns

Temple

TOWN

The Mansion

LEFT | In designing landscapes to look natural Brown used a palette of standard features. Their selection and placing depended on his judgment of the unique 'capabilities' of each place. His genius in choosing and arranging them most effectively is evident at Petworth, West Sussex. To frame, clothe and enliven parks and pleasure grounds he used various trees as specimens, clumps, belts and woodlands; also shrubberies, rolling lawns and grazed parkland. These were enclosed by walls and ha-has, and laid out with paths, drives and gateways, lakes and islands, and viewpoints. The mansion was the focus, here complemented by a temple, rotunda, boathouse, ice house and sculptural urns.

The term 'eye-catcher' is useful, as so many of his buildings did just that, whatever their main function. As ornaments they caught the eye and directed it and perhaps evoked a particular thought or mood. They were sometimes backed by and stood out palely against woodland such as Dunstall Castle above Croome. Others occupied a promontory like the Panorama Tower and Rotunda also at Croome. Another large rotunda, the Temple of Victory at Audley End, was framed by woodland in a gap so that it stood out against the sky on top of a ridge (though now it is backed by woodland on the skyline and is much less visible). Many that provided a place to shelter or sit and contemplate were embowered in shrubs. Yews formed a year-round backcloth and side screens to frame the building in the scenery, and flowering shrubs brightened and scented the scene in spring and summer.

Ruins were useful incidentals. They were best if genuinely medieval, such as Harewood Castle, Dinefwr Castle at Newton Park, and old Wardour Castle, to proclaim the pedigree of the owner (whether real or dreamed up). If the real thing was not available an authentic mock ruin could be almost as good, such as Brown's very effective Gothic Tower at Wimpole to a design by Sanderson Miller. Most of the medieval-style buildings he incorporated were not ruined: churches, stables, bridges, summerhouses, gateways. At Blenheim he designed the Keeper's Lodge and Park Farm in this style. At Burghley the elegant, south-facing Gothic orangery and Jacobean summerhouse overlook the lake. The more severe Gothic stables face the park in the other direction, the horses benefiting from the northerly aspect of the yard.

Classical temples abounded. Some are stunners, particularly at Croome, Petworth and Audley End. Park entrances were often spectacular, particularly

BELOW | Brizlee Tower, in Hulne Park, Alnwick, is one of the most spectacular buildings in Brown's many parks. It was designed by Robert Adam.

elegant ones by Robert Adam. The most splendid was his 18m (60ft) long colonnaded screen gateway looking into Syon Park, flanked by cube lodges, but his isolated London Gateway to Croome is also elegant. Holland's Roman arch stands triumphally at the entrance to the pleasure ground at Berrington, echoing the Corinthian Arch at Stowe. Quite grand menageries were built for birds and animals with pens round the back of the main building. The one at Coombe Abbey, at the far end of park, is the main eye-catcher, with other lesser buildings scattered elsewhere as lodges with archways, and so on.

Monumental columns were the ultimate in conspicuous consumption with absolutely no use other than ornamental and to the glory of the dedicatee. The visitor could slog the 30.5m (100ft) or so up an inner spiral staircase to marvel at the breath-taking view from a precarious platform or belvedere at the top. It was their role to be as prominent as possible, at least within the park and probably way beyond it. Early on Brown built the column at Stowe dedicated to Lord Cobham. He advised on the one at Gibside and designed the one at Burton Pynsent for his friend Pitt the Elder. Plenty more were put up.

Sculpture added fine art to the pleasure ground and helped to populate Brown's landscape. The choice was usually more the direct result of the taste and purse of the client. It tended to be pagan, usually Greek or Roman in flavour, rather than Christian, but rustic shepherds and shepherdesses also frolicked among the gods and their heroes, and numerous urns and vases. The density and quality of sculptures in the 1740s Grecian Valley at Stowe was exceptional but this was Lord Cobham's choice and he had a very fine eye and limitless purse. Croome too had a fine collection of lead, stone and even artificial Coade stone pieces, scattered along the pleasure ground paths at particular points to evoke various literary or historical scenes and emotions, and embellishing views. Here, they numbered sphinxes, a druid (shown left), Sabrina the reclining goddess of the River Severn, classical urns and a monument to Brown put up after his death by the 6th Earl, and plenty more.

BELOW | Sculpture added artistic interest and human figures to landscapes. The brooding Coade stone druid in the Greenhouse Shrubbery at Croome, Worcestershire, is a fine example.

Embracing the landscape: drives and views

Imagine the thrill of riding through a 'Capability' Brown park, high up on horseback or in a carriage. Whether cantering or galloping helter-skelter across the park turf or through woodland rides, or sedately trotting along admiring the scenery, listening to the birds and sniffing the country scents, the experience surely could not be beaten. Movement was essential to enjoy the constantly changing subtlety of the design in both landscape and architecture, and Brown's landscapes are anything but static.

Serpentine drives unlock the layout and planting to show off the size of the park and its variety, from carriage or saddle height. The drives to the house were ideal to express Hogarth's sought-after serpentine lines of beauty. Ashridge's Golden Valley park drive approaches along the valley side. Petworth's park drive runs along the side of a hill, elevated to show off views over the park and countryside beyond, and then a distant view of the mansion across the lake. The main drive at Milton Abbey slices through steep wooded hillside like a motorway cutting, smoothing the gradient from the two lodges at the top to the house in the valley bottom.

The owner not only enjoyed the setting himself but was out to impress guests and garden visitors with the constantly changing sequence of pictures and unpredictable experiences. Burke summed up the sensuality: 'Most people have observed the sort of sense they have had of being swiftly drawn in an easy coach on a smooth turf, with gradual ascents & declivities' (1757 *Philosophical Enquiry*.) Much earth moving was often required to obtain smooth gradients.

The landscape could even be enjoyed from the lake on boats. An excursion into the park and pleasure ground was a delight, a seductive escape into the fresh air from the controlled life indoors, and the number of routes that could be taken was endless.

Brown's drives do not generally take the shortest route, but a circuitous one on a gentle gradient. Blenheim has two great drives that contrast in mood. The one from Woodstock via the Hensington Gate has the wow factor. It is grand and spectacular, with a burst view across the valley of the magnificent scale of the palace, lake and bridge. In contrast the longer southern approach

ABOVE | A serpentine drive across the bridge displayed the buildings and landscape as visitors and family approached at Compton Verney, Warwickshire.

is lower key, its scenery Picturesque, contemplative and building to a gradual climax. Sometimes the level of the drive is slightly raised to improve the views, with a tantalising glimpse of water between the trees or a long view of the lake or palace over a concave-sloping bank. William Mavor's 1817 guide book explained the cinematic qualities of the more Picturesque and tranquil park drive:

> '…through the forest wood, which lies between [Brown's High Lodge] and the lake, [and] presents such an assemblage of views, and such various combinations of them in rapid succession, that no stranger should omit taking this route. The water, the Palace, the Gardens, the Great Bridge, the Pillar, Woodstock, and other near and remote objects, open and shut upon the eye like enchantment; and at one point, every change of a few paces furnishes a new scene, each of which would form a subject worthy of the sublimest pencil.'

Park rides were devised with similar, ever-changing effects. This was described at Croome in Dean's 1824 guide book, with its 'delightful ride, skirting the entire bounds of the domain … in a wide circuit of ten miles [with] charming prospects open, in passing, over the park…' The same effect was intended with the park perimeter rides at Ashburnham Place and Wimpole (1767). Each was defined by a serpentine avenue of trees routed over high ground to get the best views of the estate and beyond.

If left to his own devices Brown's drives approached the house obliquely in a sinuous line, so two sides of the house were seen at once (if sufficiently presentable). Otherwise the side elevation could be screened with planting. Grand axial approach avenues survived in many places, including Blenheim, Wimpole, Charlecote, Coombe Abbey, Langley Park and Corsham Court.

One of Brown's skills was to hide the surface of drives crossing the sward so that the park appeared an unbroken lawn. This was cleverly done using subtle ground modelling and is still difficult to achieve subtly, even with today's technology.

The drive was for views – trees framed and screened them, landmarks or distant hills terminated them. Brown had a hierarchy of views – from the house, garden buildings and approaches, then from park and pleasure-ground walks, rides and viewpoints. Three elements made up a view: the foreground, middle ground and distant prospect. Sometimes a view was indicated by a bend in a path marked by one or a group of exotic trees

such as London plane (Compton Verney). Views could be framed by single trees or clumps, distant views were underlined by middle-ground belts (Berrington) and undesirable features such as public roads or the ridges of hills were screened by belts. Views were often aligned on features in the wider landscape, particularly church towers and spires (Sheffield Park in Sussex) and windmills. Within the landscape viewpoints open up, such as at Coombe Abbey on hillside overlooking the long serpentine lake to the Menagerie.

'Borrowed' views between different owners' properties created the impression of a seamless single ownership, sometimes enjoyed by two parks side by side. At Prior Park Ralph Allen 'borrowed' the whole of Bath, stretched out below the sweeping parkland valley flanked by woodland. At Syon Brown's clumps and serpentine belts of trees framed views to the tidal meadow by the Thames and across the river to royal Kew, taking in elements of the two adjacent royal estates that became the present Royal Botanic Gardens. It was a diverting view, endlessly busy with river traffic, made still more eclectic after 1761 when Chambers's ten-storey Chinese Pagoda poked up above the trees in the Dowager Princess of Wales's Kew Gardens. King George III was happy to have the Syon view reciprocated when Brown laid out the riverside Richmond Gardens, adjacent to his mother's Kew estate for him in the 1760s.

ABOVE | The Grecian Valley Stowe, Buckinghamshire, was the first of Brown's magical dry valleys, with trees and shrubberies framing the vista that was intended to have a triumphal arch at the end.

FOLLOWING PAGE | Charlecote boasted two beautified rivers: one was natural (left), the other was Brown's (below). He widened and re-routed the puny Wellesbourne Brook into the Serpentine River, which sweeps through the park before cascading into the natural (though tidied up) River Avon.

Flinging open the view: the ha-ha

The ha-ha was essential in extending the view beyond the pleasure ground over the park and hiding boundaries. It defined the English Landscape Garden and Brown was a master of its use. This simple sunken device, also referred to as a fosse, surrounded the pleasure ground, allowing it to be unified with the park in views, so that no break was visible. The ha-ha was not meant to be seen and usually remained plain and self-effacing. It came from the defensive sunken fortifications used in wars of the previous century, adapted to keep out sheep and cattle as the 'enemy'. A retaining wall of brick or stone, invisible on the pleasure-ground side, allowed unbroken views into the park over a ditch that sloped gently back up on the pasture side. It could be a few metres long or hundreds of metres, straight, or preferably irregularly serpentine, in one or several sections. With its masonry and excavation costs it was expensive compared with a fence or hedge and so the longer it was, the more prestigious.

A hybrid ha-ha/wall was built at Petworth for Brown's early commission in the 1750s. The hefty stone retaining wall projected above the bank, but was low enough to allow views from the pleasure ground into the park. This rather missed the point of an invisible boundary, being reminiscent of Bridgeman's Stowe ha-ha wall. At Croome the house looks across the park towards the distant pleasure ground and Adam's great greenhouse. Brown's brick ha-ha retaining wall, although facing the house, is expertly disguised by the grading of the park ground levels in front of it. At Sandbeck, the dry-stone retaining wall divides the parkland and gardens in a curve approximately 90m (100 yards) from the house. Turning at a set of steps, it forms a bastion before running out at the woodland junction. The importance of the ha-ha to the scheme is evident from the labourers' wage book, which shows that much of the years 1771–3 was occupied in constructing ha-has around the house.

BELOW | The ha-ha opened up the view, disguising boundaries. The hybrid ha-ha/wall at Petworth, West Sussex, sticks up above ground level – rather defeating the point of an invisible barrier.

At Syon the level ground below the house is divided from the riverside tidal meadows by Brown's brick ha-ha running for over half a mile around the pleasure grounds. At Burghley Brown's local limestone ha-ha wall was designed to keep the deer herd out of the pleasure ground around the house, while maintaining uninterrupted views from the house across the park, and from the drive over the Lion Bridge back across the New River to the house.

Sunk fences did much the same thing in the park, with a fence or hedge sunk in a ditch where paddocks were invisibly divided for stock management, at less risk of damage to the animals than the steep-sided ha-ha. Brown specified park-paddock and pleasure-ground uses at Ashburnham Place, Sussex. A sunk fence and hedge survives at Wotton Underwood in the main vista some half a mile from the house. The hedge was kept low by clipping and laying and a pretty, rustic timber fence has been perpetuated.

A sheet of glistening reflective water – the jewel in the crown

A profusion of water is the most delightful and magical thing in a park, to which people gravitate as if under a spell. The highlight of a Brownian landscape is a glistening sheet of water, seemingly endless, with a plashy cascade heard and then seen. The banks wave in sinuous serpentine lines of beauty, the water held back by a dam with a craggy cascade. It was essential wherever there was even the weediest trickle of water that was reasonably constant. If possible the water was seen from the house in the middle distance. Too far away and it looked puny, too close and a wetting in the cellars was risked. To succeed, it needed the expertise of an engineer who understood the slippery nature of water, its shifty refusal to stay put without great effort, and how to thwart its frustrating inclination to emerge just where it was not wanted.

The effect of a single great silvery sheet or a never-ending serpentine river was Brown's greatest icon. Triumphantly at Blenheim, he dammed the trickling River Glyme into the vast Great Lake wrapping around below two sides of Vanbrugh's palatial mansion. It was his largest lake ever. Now Blenheim looked even more like a castle above a vast moat. Horace Walpole thought that lake was 'amazingly beautiful', praise indeed. The lake had, he thought, put the bridge's nose out of joint. Vanbrugh's huge bridge at last had a proper setting in Brown's great lake.

Such a sheet of water had coded messages: the owner was rich, for it was monumentally expensive to excavate and then to maintain; the owner had taste, for he or she had commissioned it in the latest style by the best designer; the owner was powerful in the area, for the source was obviously in his control. Size mattered, and the bigger the sheet or the wider and longer the 'river' the better. As a mirror for reflecting the house, garden buildings and trees, the surface provided an additional, ephemeral dimension to the view.

Ideally the water divided the pleasure ground from the park beyond, so that the owner could stroll by its shores on gravel paths and admire the acres of open sward, park trees and woodland beyond the silvery sheet. We see this across the lakes at Blenheim, Burghley, Croome and Longleat. Where topography was obdurate the water had to sit way out in the park, such as at Petworth, Alnwick and Wimpole. A lake could also be the venue for a detached pleasure ground, inviting an excursion from the environs of the house across the park to a sheltered walk around the water. The lake in Hatfield Forest became the detached pleasure ground for Hallingbury Place near Stansted, Essex. Rothley Lakes, similarly for Wallington some 4 miles distant, was designed as a remote, sheltered woodland lakeside walk on an otherwise windswept Northumbrian moor.

The leisured pastime of messing about in boats was popular. At Luton Hoo a sloop with ornamental sails and flying colours lay at anchor on Brown's lake. This peaked with mock naval battles, or *naumachiae*, celebrating the glory of imperial power. The 1739 *naumachia* at Cliveden had Thames barges on the river to re-enact the capture of Gibraltar. Georgian paintings of park views sometimes show model ships engaged in mock battle, complete with cannons firing.

Water took various forms and a huge sheet was not uncommon. Masterful lakes dominate at Petworth (1.3 miles long and 15 acres), Burghley (a mile long and 25 acres), Trentham (nearly a mile and some 68 acres), Harewood (½ mile long and 27 acres), Berrington (⅓ mile and 15 acres) and Gatton (½ mile long and 25 acres). Coombe Abbey is a single sheet 1½ miles long spreading over 70 acres. Luton Hoo is a similar length but divided into two sheets artfully presented as one over 55 acres, with two cascades of 3m (10ft) and 9m (30ft). But the granddaddy of them all has to be Blenheim at 1½ miles long and 115 acres in extent as a single sheet all at the same level.

BELOW | Water is the most precious and sought-after element in the park. At Croome, Worcestershire, Brown engineered both a mile-long river and a lake, and, as his monument notes, 'formed this garden scene out of a morass'.

Park lakes were meant to be read as rivers. Where a river did not exist the art was in making a lake look like a broad, winding, endless river. Some remarkably convincing 'rivers' were created in valley bottoms at places such as Coombe Abbey and Luton Hoo. Even the Great Lake at Blenheim was regarded by the Georgians as having the 'bold shores of a noble river'. Ideally the view conjured up visions to the initiated of the Rivers Tiber or Arno of classical Italy.

A linear river generally required less earth moving than a broad sheet of water. It was easier to keep filled and looking good, and left more park sward for grazing. Brown magicked up many. At Wimpole the merest trickle of water was expanded into three lakes over 10 acres to resemble the River Cam heading for Cambridge, and at Audley End the real River Cam was widened in front of the house to make it more impressive. At Croome the canalised park drainage outflow pretended convincingly to be the River Severn. The nakedness of Brown's river banks provoked some criticism, but there is a certain satisfaction in the contrast between smooth solid sward and the sinuous line of the water beyond.

Charlecote had two rivers, one artificial, the other natural. The 'Serpentine River' was created out of the puny Wellesbourne Brook and ran through the park before it cascaded into the natural (though tidied up) River Avon. As well as widening the Brook, Brown subtly altered its course, moving it away from the house and stables and to enhance their setting. The new Serpentine River was ornamented with trees, including fine oak and London plane specimens that still grace the scene.

Natural rivers were valued and sometimes enlarged or diverted. At Newton Park (Dinefwr Castle) the River Towy caught the eye from the drive along the edge of the plateau, snaking across the plain far away below. The Derwent at Chatsworth was tamed, widened and its banks graded and a classical James Paine bridge thrown over it. Nuneham Courtenay overlooked the sublime reach of the Thames just below Oxford, and took advantage of views of both, framing the edge of the park below the classical house.

At Alnwick, the River Aln was tamed as Brown transformed a feisty moorland stream into a sedate river below the Percys' medieval castle. The Duke of Northumberland had made plans for a vast lake as great as any in England, on which the pioneering canal engineer James Brindley advised, but after a tumultuous flood in 1771 it was deemed imprudent. The river had to do as the main water, a role it fulfilled well in the newly artified park setting. Brindley advised on a series of cascades to slow the flow of water so it could be broadened to a serene ribbon. The graceful, three-arched, crenellated Lion Bridge spanned it, its Gothic appearance complementing the rugged castle above. It remains dominated by a lead figure of the Percys' life-size heraldic lion with outstretched tail. Brown built a high terrace overlooking

BELOW | Brown widened the River Cam below the house at Audley End, Essex, to make it more impressive, with Robert Adam's elegant road bridge thrown over it (Edmund Garvey, 1782).

the new river and a small part of the surrounding huge parks that he helped to fashion. Despite the lack of a decently expansive lake the Duke imported a sailing boat from the south of England, which spent the summer sailing up and down the rather constricted stretch of the river below the castle.

Some places offered the opportunity for both lakes and rivers. Croome has both Brown's pleasure-ground lake, surrounded by sculpture and garden buildings, and the fairly convincing version of the River Severn snaking for a mile across the park. Syon House trumps this with a mile-long reach of the mighty Thames, symbol of British trade at the heart of the Empire, as well as two Brown lakes. The park is dominated by Lancelot Brown's second (4-acre, ⅓ mile long) sheet of water, with an iron bridge that replaced the original by Robert Adam. In the wooded pleasure ground he had previously dug the ⅓-mile-long Serpentine River.

Brown was generally regarded as a master with water. He grasped new engineering techniques available for land drainage, particularly effectively used in East Anglia, and canals. Improvement in surveying and levelling equipment probably helped to increase the scope for previously impossibly extensive water schemes in serpentine lakes. He accomplished a major feat when he fixed the level of the lake at Blenheim in 1765 to suit Vanbrugh's bridge, partly submerging it, even though it could not be seen from the top of the dam. Despite these great strides, the spadework was, literally, enormous.

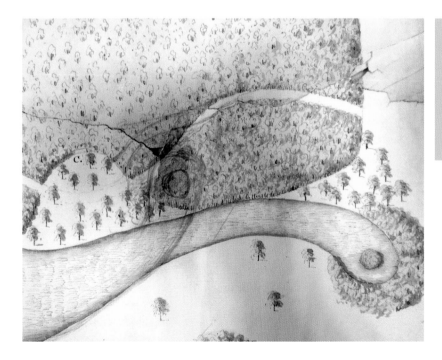

LEFT | The 1757 plan of Hatfield Forest, Essex, shows Brown's alternative schemes for the end of the lake, each with an island obscuring it, enclosed by woodland to make it seem like an endless river.

Drainage, although far from sexy, was a major preoccupation for the estate owner. Many of Brown's schemes required major drainage networks. A handy and prestigious receptacle to carry away the drained water was an ornamental sheet of water. From Brown's earliest jobs improvement to drainage, especially in the environs of the mansion, was a key to successful park design. Croome and Petworth had extensive drainage networks feeding their new waters. In 1824 the writer of the Croome guidebook comments: 'while the stranger stands, admiring the winding waters, refreshing and adorning the meads, through which they take their way – he ought to be informed that this is the grand receptacle of the numerous drains, which have given, to the whole surrounding tract, all its beauty, and all its value.' The monument erected to Brown's memory by Lord Coventry at Croome, paid tribute to this skill, praising how he had 'formed this garden scene/ out of a morass'. It is sometimes possible to see the outfall of an underground stone or brick-lined conduit draining into the lake. These conduits could be up to 90cm (3ft) in diameter and are prone to collapse if disturbed by heavy machinery.

ABOVE | Brown's impressive culverts at Croome were invisible but essential to turn bog into parkland, and to fill new rivers and lakes.

Puddled clay lined the new basin to make it watertight. A blanket of 'well temper'd clay' was bucketed by hand over the lake bottom as a lining. It was tamped down by men with rammers, it is said in some places using the cloven hoofs of sheep driven across it to key it to the ground below. The clay was extra thick at the edges to prevent cracking if the banks were exposed in summer when the water level fell.

The dam is critical in any of these water schemes. This could involve major earthworks or be more subtle. The waters at Blenheim, Burghley and Berrington are held back by high dams with impressive banks. Brown's earth dams were usually covered on the lakeside against the body of water with a

blanket of clay. This clay was in turn covered by a layer of stones to protect it from the lapping of water and vermin burrowing into it. At Blenheim the Grand Cascade was further strengthened by a clay core, an established technique in fenland flood banks. The dam was an interesting place to route the circuit walk as at Berrington and Wotton Underwood. At Wotton low graded banks holding the water back stretch almost imperceptibly for hundreds of metres and in places are used for the circuit path. At Wycombe Abbey, the narrow, 6-acre lake, now the focus of High Wycombe's Rye recreation ground, is a *tour de force* of embankment skill, perching ½ mile of sinuous water on a hillside just above the River Wye.

The water outlet was ideal for the splashy noise and picturesque appearance of a cascade over the top of the dam, but this could weaken the structure. Blenheim has one of Brown's most impressive cascades but there are many

ABOVE | Rothley Upper Lake, Northumberland has an impressive dam.

others. The downstream side of the dam, where not incorporating a cascade, would be turfed in a gently concave bank or planted with a shrubbery and trees to disguise it. Sluices regulated the height of the water and released water safely. A pipe through the bottom of the dam allowed water to be evacuated in a regulated way into the watercourse below.

Tricks of the design trade gently deceived the viewer into believing these glinting sheets of water were natural, not the product of huge amounts of sweat and toil. To make the water seem endless Brown used curves to conceal the ends from each other, so that the whole sheet was not visible in one sweeping view. The natural topography could help, as at Coombe Abbey and Patshull, which are L- and J-shaped respectively. At Coombe Abbey the valley turns a dog leg twice and Brown managed a mile-and-a-half long *tour de force*. Islands at the ends or part-way along were useful where a kink would not work to stop the ends being seen in one sweep, as at Wotton Underwood and Hatfield Forest. As well as screening, islands framed views at Berrington, Wotton and Petworth. They were convenient places for some of the spoil from digging the lake and to position buildings or sculpture. The main island in the lake at Wotton Underwood has a grotto and that at Petworth has a stone urn.

Even the unavoidable changes of level of several stretches of water were expertly concealed. At Gayhurst, Buckinghamshire, one visitor was impressed (but ultimately not deceived!) for, 'The water in the park, though it consists of several pieces of different levels, has the effect of being in one single sheet when seen from the house: this was very ingeniously executed by Mr. Brown'.

Sham bridges concealed the artificiality of dams and changing water levels, and sometimes planting too. At Wimpole a clump of trees disguises the dam between the lakes across the park in the vista between the mansion and Sanderson Miller's Sham Castle put up by Brown. A line of billowing pale green London plane trees on the dam draws the eye over the water to the Gothic Ruin. Unfortunately the water is concealed from the house in a dip between it and the Ruin but the Ruin is beautifully elevated to draw the eye from the house.

Bridges carried drives and roads as well as disguising dams and changes in level. At Burghley, Brown's three-arched stone bridge carries the main drive over his New River (really a lake). A similar bridge at Compton Verney may be by him or Adam, and the same conundrum as to bridge authorship occurs at Syon. Elegant bridges in pleasure grounds appeared too, such as the covered timber Palladian Bridge at Scampston, Yorkshire.

Not everything went swimmingly for Brown and water though. He knew how fickle this element could be, a lesson learnt early on at Stowe with the resolutely dry Grecian Valley. After 20 years the river at Croome leaked due to tree-root damage and Lord Coventry asked for Brown's man to return to fix the problem. There were also problems with earthworks at Petworth and Burghley.

The park

GRAZED LAWNS AND TURF: THE PARK FLOOR

The park offered a wide-open, rolling landscape. It contained smooth greensward, trees, drives and stock to graze it. In the painterly terms of the time it formed the offskip from the house – that part of a landscape, which recedes from the spectator into the distance. It was often substantially walled with local stone or brick, or fenced. Blenheim, Croome and Petworth have fine park walls. The height of the stone wall at Appuldurcombe House on the Isle of Wight varies to suit local topography. Elaborate gateways were built for the family and important visitors, and service entrances for staff, often marked with lodges standing guard.

For the sake of the whole design and the owner's privacy public roads and footpaths were sometimes moved. The extent of the park and unity of Brown's design at Syon Park were limited until the road to Isleworth was diverted away. The main road was moved at Luton Hoo beyond the lake, hidden by a belt of trees. Other owners were happy to embrace public roads in the park design, but at a distance from the house. Berrington has a main road slicing across the park. Audley End has two, one carried by a fancy bridge by Adam, and several public footpaths across it. At Milton Abbey the whole town was removed, because it stood inconveniently close to the house, and a model village was built by Brown to replace it as a park feature.

ABOVE AND BELOW | Deer were prestigious in park views. Jagged fencing discouraged them from jumping out and was ornamental too. Charlecote Park, Warwickshire.

Earth movement was part of the process, but the less obvious the better. It was often at a vast scale with dozens of men employed in winter wielding shovels, pickaxes and wheelbarrows. Huge amounts of effort and labour went into smoothing off slopes at Petworth and Blenheim, particularly around lakes, and to accommodate drives cut into hillsides, making mounds to screen features, or platforms for clumps as at Gatton. At the King's Richmond Gardens Brown's 1773 excavations, originally called the Hollow Walk, survive in the present Kew Gardens as the Rhododendron Dell.

The park floor is now taken for granted, but the uniform greenness alongside smooth land forms and waving lines was another part in the appreciation of beauty in the landscape. Greensward was a major element. Lawns were prestigious and not restricted to the garden and pleasure ground. Park lawns were important, not just as a backdrop. Often the house was fronted by a sweeping expanse of empty park lawn, which showed off livestock and well-bred horses. At Petworth, pasture that ran right up to the door of the mansion in its most magnificent façade was grazed by the herd of fallow deer. Internal fences and other boundaries were kept to a minimum to perpetuate the sense of endless space.

Nothing beats the sight of a great Brownian park valley framed in woodland, even though there is no sheet of water at all. The Grecian Valley at Stowe, the Golden Valley at Ashridge and the sweeping valleys of Milton Abbey all

RIGHT | Dry valleys were as much part of Brown's designs as lakes. Smoothly curving slopes led up to trees containing pleasure-ground paths on the upper slopes which hid the ridges. This is the Golden Valley, Ashridge, Hertfordshire.

are masterpieces fashioned from otherwise unpromising, even barren, sites. The brows of the flanking ridges are clothed in deciduous woodland, which comes fingering down the valley side in crinkly lines. At Stowe, Whately, writing in 1770, admired the way the 'lovely woods and groves hang all the way on the declivities; and the open space is broken by detached trees ... as the valley sinks they advance more boldly down the sides, stretch across or along the bottom, and cluster at times into groups or forms, which multiply the varieties of the larger plantations ... the trees rise in one upon high stems, and feather down to the bottom in another...'

The term 'lawnde' originated as a grassy clearing in woodland; clearings or lawn became an essential part of the greensward of the Brownian landscape park and one finds in records 'lawn down to the water', 'lawns to the downs'. Grass seeding was important, especially in more remote areas, rather than turfing, which was done near the house. At Petworth, having drained and levelled 'all such parts as are intended to grass throughout the whole designe', Brown sowed the area with clean, dressed hay seed and Dutch clover. The turf was grazed by sheep, cattle, horses or even deer, or mown for hay at midsummer and then grazed to dung it. More horses were kept in the eighteenth century as travel and sport developed, and equine breeding took off from hunting and racing, so more grass was needed to feed them.

CLOTHING THE PARK IN PLANTS

Trees punctuated Brown's park sward in singles, clumps and copses to frame views, screen unwanted scenes, provide shade and emphasise land form. Once scattered with trees land could not easily be converted from pasture to arable, for ploughing around them was difficult. The trees broke the force of the wind and improved the climate for growing sward, more so if the park was encircled by a woodland belt. Returning to Brown's own grammatical analogy, they punctuated a particular point, in a fold of the park, on the brow of a hill, on either side of the approach drive, or screening untidy buildings.

Belts and woods were useful and versatile. They contained extensive circuit rides, sheltered the park trees and sward, were the source of timber for estate use and to sell, and screened the outside world. Not all Brown's parks have perimeter belts and woodland but, when he used them he did so to great artistic effect, perhaps most effectively to outline the brow of surrounding hills. He planted the barren downland hills at Milton Abbey with undulating woodland, creating promontories above the open park.

The trees were generally deciduous natives – conifer plantations were not widely used except to nurse deciduous trees as they got established. For example, Brown advised Lord Bute at Highcliffe to establish belts of Scotch firs and pines around the cliff-top house. These, once grown up a bit, could then be used to shelter other trees, protecting them from the searing salt-laden winds of the English Channel. Game birds favour woodland edges against open land, so narrow belts gave plenty of these edges to encourage them for sporting owners. Blenheim has a belt alongside its park wall, while Brown's park at Wimpole is sheltered by belts on the surrounding slopes. At Berrington the park ride is just outside the belt, enjoying the best views to the distant countryside.

Brown's park planting was a palette of largely native forest trees, chosen depending on local conditions. Oak, sycamore, lime, ash, elm and beech in open parkland grew to be magnificent specimens. Hawthorn was a valued smaller tree. Mingling species was thought to be more cheerful, but often clumps and loose groves were of a single type. Having assessed what seemed to thrive locally Brown planted accordingly. So in the northern Chilterns at Ashridge, Beechwood and Luton Hoo he used many beech, oak and ash. He used other types such as Scots pine and planes but as specimen trees or as the dominant tree at the centre of a clump.

Beech was a signature tree at Blenheim, where many fine old specimens survive, particularly a grove around Fair Rosamund's Well by the lake,

ABOVE | The careful placing of trees is essential to the design of a park and its views. Imagine this park at Newton House (Dinefwr Castle), Wales, without the trees – it would not exist.

together with giant Lebanon cedars, all seen beyond the lake from the forecourt. Elms were a great feature and we often forget how much the landscape has changed with their loss since the 1970s. Long-established exotics such as horse chestnut and sweet chestnut were also used.

Variety came from showy exotics among the reliable natives. Varied colour and form was important. Contrasting shades of green showed off the painterly effects of light and shade, distancing objects by framing them with lighter leaf colour and making things seem further away. The billowing form of pale London plane particularly stood out against darker evergreens and the specimens are now so much more striking than could ever have been the case in Brown's time. The small, pale leaves of the false acacia trembled in the breeze with extravagant white racemes of flowers in early summer.

Brown made the darkly evergreen, layered Lebanon cedar his own. It has been said that no tree introduced to Britain has added more to the charm of gardens than the Lebanon cedar. Sadly, Brown's cedars are close to reaching their life span of some 250–300 years. But some noble specimens do survive and should be treasured. As well as the grove around Fair Rosamund's Well, Brown's cedars still grace Croome and Compton Verney. Lebanons, like the

London plane, are not keen on the northern climate and prefer warmer parts of Britain. Introduced around the 1670s they were treasured as noble exotics, achieving a distinctive crown of wide-spreading layers of branches that looks quite different from trees in their native habitat.

The London plane was another Brown trademark and seems to have proved more robust than the fragile Lebanon cedar. Its origin is hazy as a hybrid, with the Oriental plane as one of its parents, introduced in the late seventeenth or early eighteenth century. Its noble outline, with a soaring trunk and distinctive crinkly framework of branches in the crown above, is clothed in pale green, hand-shaped, leathery leaves.

The planes we see today suggest that Brown used them sparingly, though he ordered dozens at a time for some of his schemes such as at Petworth. At both Compton Verney and Latimer a single magnificent specimen stands

next to the main drive where it crosses the water on a carriage bridge. A plane with other specimen trees flanks Hiorn's bridge for the main road at Charlecote. Another, now lost, marked the cascade at Blenheim. In one of his last schemes, of *c.*1780, four planes at Berrington line one side of a view towards the triumphal arch gateway, and a wobbly line of nine or so planes on the dam at Wimpole frames the view towards the Gothic Tower and disguises the change in water level between lakes. One of around 1773 stands proudly at the head of Brown's sunken Hollow Walk in Kew Gardens. In contrast to these set self-effacingly in the middle or far distance, a vast specimen plane at Chalfont Park is set right outside the front door, just offset from the central view. Several other, more modest planes are scattered in the park nearby. Brown had vision indeed to plant these majestic trees, and to imagine how they would eventually stand in a commanding position. He does not seem to have been a fan of the dark copper beech, nor of the hybrid Lucombe oak, which became popular elsewhere.

BELOW | The Greenhouse Shrubbery pleasure ground at Croome had a vibrant botanical and floral display in and around the Temple Greenhouse, overlooking the ha-ha to the distant mansion.

Evergreens were valued in winter, to banish the deathly season, to a degree that we cannot comprehend today. The Scots pine (in Brown's time called the Scotch fir) was a popular evergreen choice, but few survive. The old Caledonian form has a bluey-green spreading canopy and loses its lower branches above the distinctive red-hued bark. Other conifers included Norway spruce and European larch. Conifers were possibly used as 'nurses' in plantations, but Brown's plans show them scattered across the parkland turf as an evergreen element of variety in colour and form, and along the margins of plantations such as at Burton Constable. Here the large numbers of native deciduous trees and exotic conifers were supplemented with thousands of silver birch, as well as American sugar maples and scarlet oaks. Holm oak was a good choice, but few survive. Sometimes a mistake was made. The clumps of firs Brown specified at Latimer didn't last long on the Chiltern chalk soil. Yews were not grown in parkland as they were poisonous to livestock, even though their sombre hues were much valued in pleasure grounds.

Young trees came from a nursery on the estate or a nurseryman. Brown was adept at transplanting challengingly large trees; this was common while he was at Stowe and he used his ingenuity. While working there he planted thousands of trees, including elm, beech and Scots pine. Many were transplanted at quite a size, some from other parts of the place, including

BELOW | The Cedar of Lebanon is Brown's iconic signature tree, with its unique layered form.

the Grecian Valley. To do this he used, possibly invented, a tree carriage to lift them out of the ground and take them to their new home. The accounts refer to large limes and elms transplanted from other parts of the estate. The single, very large London plane at the far end of the Grecian Valley may also be his; a pale sentinel above the ha-ha, it survives in stately form with a soaring trunk.

Shrubs were planted in the park, but seldom survive. At Petworth laurel and other low-growing ornamentals were planted on the margins of plantations and as 'plantations of low shrubs'. These may have sheltered the young trees, and must have been fenced to keep the fallow deer herd from destroying them completely.

For Petworth Brown bought from Williamson the nurseryman evergreen Scots pine, Norway spruce and over 200 cedar of Lebanon. Deciduous trees included larch, dozens of planes, false acacias and limes. The boundary was planted with a 'plantation of shrubs and plants of low growth; that will not prevent the prospect' out across the countryside. These have all but gone, leaving a much simplified framework.

Fine veteran trees from earlier landscapes were often kept, particularly the long-lived English oak and sweet chestnut, and many still survive. Blenheim, Burghley and Petworth parks as well as Hatfield and Savernake Forest are all special for this continuity, depth of age and amazing character of the trees. In 1770 the Duchess of Northumberland noted in her travel diary that the park at Petworth was 'extreamly well-wooded with the finest trees imaginable.' In particular, 'The Chestnuts, Oaks, & Beeches are of a stupendous size & surpass all that I have seen in my life.' Brown's work was less than 20 years old at this point, so she must have been talking of the long-established park trees.

Still more of his parks have species introduced since his day. Atlantic (blue) cedars (Blenheim has a fine collection), deodar cedars, Corsican pine and the ubiquitous and fast-growing Wellingtonia (or Giant Redwood) are later additions that he did not have available. The uncompromisingly pyramidal and massively evergreen Wellingtonia is probably the most alien. Introduced from America in 1853 just after the Iron Duke's death, it is now reaching a vast size and form in Brown's landscapes, which jars with his concepts, disrupting that sense of unity and calm, in which nothing disturbs the eye. More sensitively, a magnificent Wellingtonia avenue at Compton Verney is discretely shrouded on the edge of the pleasure ground. Its potential for visual mayhem in Brown's design, particularly competing with the Lebanon cedars near the house and lake, is quietly suppressed behind woodland.

Playgrounds: the pleasure ground

The pleasure ground was a more intimate environment for dallying and dalliance in fresh air. It was convenient for walking straight out of the house and enjoying gentle exercise and views from gravel and grass paths, rather than the more robust park. It was particularly suited to damp days and those with long skirts, and delicate shoes and constitutions. The pleasure ground contained lawns, beautiful and scented flowers, engaging buildings and sculpture, linked by winding paths. Sometimes, such as at Petworth, it contained a more highly cultivated flower garden and conservatory, perhaps a greenhouse or hothouse stove too. Although we tend to think that Brown abolished the flower garden, this is wrong. He did design flower gardens, but they were usually discretely enclosed, secret and hidden from wider view.

A plethora of garden buildings was available. Summerhouse temples (Burghley, Blenheim, Petworth), menageries (Uppark), grottoes (Croome, Clandon), and perhaps a bason or other water feature (Uppark). The east garden pleasure ground at Wallington contained a pinery (a hot house for growing pineapples), shrubberies, plantations and other ornaments.

Brown was as creative at pleasure grounds as he was at parks. He often produced the two together, but for this more intricate design work he is less well known. Winding walks led out as far as the park or to the kitchen garden. Some appeared to stop in thin air at the edge of the pleasure ground as the circuit walk crossed part of the park without benefit of a dry-shod

RIGHT | Dark trees frame the pale stone Owl Seat at Croome to make it more prominent when viewed from the house over half a mile away.

gravel path, as in the Lowther designs. A pleasure ground was often based on an earlier ornamental Wilderness, modifying existing formal groves with paths cut through them around informal shrubberies. Serpentine paths had beds fitted into their shapes.

The pleasure ground came in various forms. Most common was a compact shrubbery with lawns alongside the house. Otherwise the choice was a circuit walk sweeping in a great loop enclosing grazed paddocks. Petworth and Uppark were compact, self-contained and close to the house. For the more energetic Wotton Underwood has one of those sweeping circuit walks from the house, some 2½ miles long, taking in the lakes, rivers and paddocks of a *ferme ornée*. A shorter circuit cuts it to just under 2 miles, but it is not for the faint-hearted or poorly shod. The park proper was beyond this. Croome, like Stowe, had several shrubberies, all linked on the 2-mile circuit walk arcing around and across the park.

Brown could adapt his formula to any scale, as Cadland (created *c.*1775) in Hampshire shows. It is a little gem: one of his best surviving sites where the design was carried out according to the plan, still showing us his intentions. For this client, Robert Drummond, his banker, Brown's solution for the pleasure ground was a miniature landscape park, complete with perimeter belts, sheltered circuit walks, clumps and scattered trees.

Because of the confined 15-acre site he based the layout on a shrubbery circuit walk in scale with Holland's ornamental fishing lodge by the Solent (then called Boarn Hill Cottage). Continuous wooded shrubbery backed the walk, with occasional carefully contrived views glimpsing the sea and more frequent views into the home 'paddock'. The paddock was not for stock but was an ornamental lawn planted with shrub beds and individual specimens. A terraced walk cut into the bank above the beach was marked on his plan as 'The Sea Bank with a Path of Gravell amongst the Furze Bushes etc'. The route back to the house was via 'A Path or Walk under the Hedge with Shrubs and Plants that will Grow'. His formal flower garden adjacent to the walk was divided into quarters and screened by a belt of shrubbery.

The Wilderness Walk at Syon Park (1750s, modified 1767–70) was by contrast long and wavy. It meandered from the house towards the church between a band of screening shrubbery and large detached shrubbery clumps, overlooking lawns sloping down to the ha-ha above the flood meadows and the Thames beyond. At the other extreme of the scale, Croome, Wotton Underwood and Brown's Walk at Newton Park (Dinefwr) were based on extensive circuit walks from the house around stock paddocks with views back to the house.

Walks were carefully routed and constructed. Grass paths were for the summer, and gravel walks came into their own in winter. Croome had

BELOW | The Temple of Concord and Victory at Stowe is one of the largest garden buildings, dominating Brown's Grecian Valley. It is both a focal point from many parts of the valley and a viewpoint from which to survey the scene.

both. At Burton Constable in East Yorkshire gravel walks of 1.8–2.4m (6–8ft) wide were made.

CLOTHING THE PLAYGROUND IN PLANTS

Much of the pleasure in the pleasure ground was to be had from the delightful planting. Flower and leaf colour, leaf form and fragrance were keenly appreciated. Most pleasure grounds contained shrubberies of deciduous flowering or evergreen species, often segregated to one or the other. Plants were set out singly rather than in groups of a single type, which only came into fashion in the early nineteenth century. Borders were banded with bulbs, annuals and perennials. Sometimes shrubs were elevated on banks to help screen anything undesirable. An evergreen spine or backdrop to the bed was useful for this too.

Trees that Brown used included natives from the park, particularly English oak, elm, beech and sweet chestnut. Yew was a favourite evergreen native, as here it could not be got at by livestock, and again Scots pine. Exotics included Holm oak, European larch, stone and Austrian pines and Norway spruce, mixed with American conifers and oaks. Italian cypress, Far Eastern *Ginkgo*, and American tulip tree and false acacia were other popular exotics seldom seen today. Lebanon cedars often framed the house, with London planes near water, especially bridges.

At Hatfield Forest in Essex a great plane and oak stand paired on the lake bank near the Shell House and another plane marks the end of Brown's single executed river (one of two) marking the outfall. Several massive yews and Scots pine line the bank of his 'river'. Two huge dark yews with peculiar striated trunks closely flank the Gothic Ruin at Milton Abbey, across the park from the mansion.

In Brown's pleasure grounds today much of the planted variety has gone, as in his parks. Those plants that do survive below the tree canopy are the robust species: Portuguese and cherry laurel, yew, box, butcher's broom and holly.

The main flowering season was limited by the palette available. Lady Luxborough of Barrells noted that flowering shrubs were 'in their prime'

around Whitsun, with perennials and annuals at their best in July and August. Snowdrops and polyanthus were appreciated in spring. Even so seasonal interest could be extended, using evergreen foliage and recently introduced North American plants. The season started with pinky-white-flowering and evergreen laurustinus in winter, cherry laurel, arbor vitae (*Thuja occidentalis*), holm oak (*Quercus ilex*), Daphne in February, pink almond in March, hawthorns in April/May.

The main flowering season was in April to June. May was lilac-tide with lilacs in variety, double thorn trees and yellow laburnums. A favourite combination that seems rather bright today was lilacs, laburnum and white guelder rose. Roses came in June, with honeysuckle, yellow broom, mock orange and the false acacia's white wells. Later in the season came the colourful red American *Campsis radicans* vine and the Indian bean tree with its white flowers and long dry black pods in autumn and winter came into their own.

Roses were prized, even though there was only a small selection of species with few varieties, and the flowering season was restricted to early summer without repeat flowering. A bill for Petworth dated March 1756 lists 100 roses: 60 Sweet Briar, 5 Rosa Mundi, 5 Maidens Blush, 6 double White, 3 Belgick, 6 Damask, 5 Virgin, 6 Province, 6 Monthly, 4 York and Lancaster.

The same trees and shrubs were often used in both park and pleasure ground to unite the two across the ha-ha. The trademark cedars of Lebanon are used at many places in both the pleasure ground and in the park, such as at Blenheim and Compton Verney. So too were London planes, either singly, in groups or in lines. The paler yellow-green leaved trees were good to alter perspective, including the tulip tree, western, Oriental and London planes, and weeping willow, when seen against the darker evergreens of Portuguese laurel and yew. He was happy to use weeping willow at Tottenham when Lord Bruce was able to procure some – he thought would be 'Picturesque and in the taste of the Forest Birch Trees' when scattered about. Cascading weeping willow were planted as specimens on the Temple Lawn near Garrick's Shakespeare Temple on the bank of the Thames, contrasting with dark needle-like Italian cypress.

Brown used exotics in both pleasure grounds and parks, but he is not known to have favoured a wide selection. At Syon House the long shrubbery walk –

the Church Walk Wilderness – was planted with a range of shrubs including evergreen honeysuckles, Alexandrian laurels, lilacs, laburnums, mock orange and viburnums. Six cedars were also planted here.

Newly imported American species were all the rage, with some owners becoming obsessed with collecting them. Many American introductions came with nurseryman John Bartram's boxes of seeds sent over to wealthy subscribers. Petworth in the 1750s was supplied with American plants including Virginia sumach, Virginia raspberry, fragrant candleberry, *Cotinus coggygria*, catalpa, American maples, campsis, false acacia and western plane. At Burton Constable in 1775 Brown's scheme was supplemented with 37 sorts of American seeds from Sigston's nursery, Beverley, but he does not seem to have been a great promoter of these introductions in his schemes.

The peculiar Georgian fascination for the evergreen shrubbery is explained in the Croome guide book of 1824. The evergreen shrubbery banished the desolation of winter, which they were forced to endure unless they were able to travel south on the Grand Tour. Evergreens Brown typically used included cedar of Lebanon (ultimately huge), Norway spruce, hemlock, Scots pine (our only native pine), stone and Weymouth pines, arbor vitae (white cedar), Italian cypress (doubtfully hardy), holly, phillyrea (seldom seen today), laurustinus (a viburnum), 'striped' and plain box, bay, arbutus, common juniper, myrtle, evergreen oak, cherry and Portuguese laurel. His evergreens seem rather pedestrian or even unsuitable for our own gardens, but he was working on a different scale and with a limited palette.

BELOW | A Wilderness was a pleasure-ground shrubbery of delightful buildings, plants and views. Brown's Church Walk at Syon Park (top left), was a long wavy walk above a ha-ha overlooking the Thames and Royal Botanic Gardens Kew, and led the family to church (Rocque Map of Middlesex, c.1766).

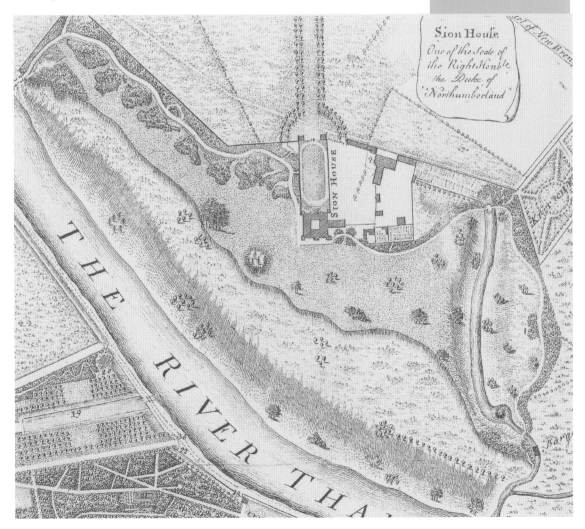

CHAPTER 4

Brown's
buildings

Fame as an architect

Brown was a competent and renowned architect of many building types. His designs offer a snapshot of the myriad buildings owners were commissioning in their grounds. Memory of his prowess as an architect has faded but he was the creator of excellent country houses, estate buildings and many beguiling park structures. To complement his country-house landscapes, where required he designed mansions and stable blocks, and park buildings, including summerhouses and churches, bridges and chapels. Less ornamentally he built kitchen gardens, ha-has, humble ice houses and still more humble (but vital) culverts and drains. Some believe that Brown designed his parks with fewer buildings as time went on, but this is not quite so. He also worked alongside other architects and many of their buildings were designed as eye-catchers at particular places in his scenes.

Brown's buildings are not given much attention today, but in his own time he had a considerable reputation as an architect. This was quickly forgotten, for as Humphry Repton, Brown's successor from the 1790s as the most famous name in landscaping, explained only 20 years after Brown's death, 'Mr Brown's fame as an architect seems to have been eclipsed by his

PREVIOUS PAGE | Brown's complete design service included buildings, as he was an able architect. At Croome, Worcestershire, in the 1750s, he built the country house and stables within the park and designed the new church.

BELOW | Claremont, Surrey, where Brown designed both the house and park for 'nabob' Clive of India at a cost of over £30,000.

celebrity as a landscape gardener', as he was 'the only professor of the one art, while he had many jealous competitors in the other'. His buildings were successful because they were imbued with 'the higher requisites of the art relating to *form*, to *proportion*, to *character*, and above all to *arrangement*'.

Brown placed some fine buildings in his landscapes to rival those of the big-name architects of the day, such as Robert Adam and James Wyatt. The mansion at Claremont stands up against the best of any of the period, and there is still his beautiful album of designs for it, signed by both him and Clive of India in 1771 (drawn up by John Ashby). He was not a jobbing architect, mostly designing in country-house estates and in association with his landscaping schemes. Repton enthused about his buildings, particularly the 'comfort, convenience, taste and propriety of design in the several mansions and other buildings which he planned'.

At Stowe in the 1740s Brown had realised that architecture was a useful string to his bow and he worked with great architects, learning building techniques and how to run complex contracts. After Stowe much of his work was built by Henry Holland, a master builder of Fulham. Holland's son Henry worked as an architect with Brown from 1771, giving the younger man a good start to his own successful career. In 1774 Henry junior married Brown's daughter Bridget.

From the 1750s many owners employed the swanky architects of the day at Brown's sites. These men emerged with new creative ideas as Britain prospered. William Chambers, Robert Adam, James Paine and James Wyatt, who worked on many of the same estates as Brown, turned their backs on the heavy Baroque of Vanbrugh's Blenheim and Burlington's Palladian style in favour of the Neo-classical. Many had travelled on the Continent or beyond on Grand Tours, and introduced a new pictorial richness into architecture, including landscape structures. Their inventive classicism conveyed movement in the facades as part of the scenic composition.

In many cases these architects designed a suite of garden buildings too, as did Adam at Croome, and some garden buildings at different parks are surprisingly similar. There is often confusion about the designer of buildings in Brown's parks, whether it was him or the other architect who was also working there, especially where no documentation survives. At Alnwick, within Brown's framework, the Duke of Northumberland commissioned three park buildings in memory of his wife (*d.*1776) who was passionate about ruins and garden buildings: the Observatory, the Summerhouse at the ruined Hulne Priory, and the frothy six-storey Brizlee Tower on a

blowy hilltop, a stunning, soaring park landmark in a rare example of Adam's Gothic. These were apparently the product of a somewhat uneasy collaboration between Adam, Brown and the Duke's gardeners.

At Audley End Adam devised the suite of garden buildings over two decades including the Temple of Victory on Ring Hill, the Palladian bridge (similar to Brown's version at Scampston) and tea house (both 1782–3). The three-arched bridge at Audley End (1764), attributed to Adam, is very similar to Brown's bridge at Burghley, and his design for the one at Ashburnham Place in Sussex.

Georgian mansions – comfort, convenience, taste and design

Brown's career took off just as sensational changes hit the architecture of country houses in tandem with the new informal design of their grounds. These changes were driven by the new way that 'polite society' lived and enjoyed themselves. By the 1750s, when Brown set up on his own, 'formal' plans for great houses were out. With the improvement in roads and carriages, visiting friends in country houses became an enjoyable pastime for the wealthy and helped to spur the development of a new style of house. Social customs of the elite no longer required a sequence of rooms leading progressively more privately to the most intimate and sought-after presence chamber of the owner or his wife. Instead, the host wished to let guests stroll through a circuit of equally interesting reception rooms reached from a central core. The circuit of rooms was better suited to informal social encounters than the old Baroque 'axis of honour'. Entertaining was less formal, separating the company into more intimate groups in various rooms for amusements such as cards and dancing. Each room was open to guests and family alike. The sequence provided a distinct experience indoors while also embracing the landscape beyond.

The hall, which had been so important socially and a place to eat meals, became little more than an entrance room. A separate dining room became the norm instead. As with the company, so elegance and gaiety guided the décor. The hall was often decorated in a neutral pale stone colour that evoked a Roman atrium, but once the visitor moved into the social rooms on the circuit they were enveloped in a series of dazzling hues of pink, blue, yellow and green especially popularised by Adam. Each room was designed as a distinct experience with views of the park from a variety of constantly changing angles. Private apartments remained important but were no longer the most prestigious part of the house.

ABOVE | Brown carefully positioned buildings in his landscapes, framed among the park and woodland. The house was often the main eye-catcher, as at Berrington Hall, Herefordshire (seen centre left).

It is obvious when visiting a country house that the owner wanted us to admire the decor and exquisite collection of *objets d'art* in the main rooms. But as much as this he wanted us to turn to the windows and gaze out into the fashionable new landscape garden by Brown. The house and grounds were a single work of art and fashion dictated that the inside should meet the outside.

The use of the interiors may not seem relevant to the landscape, but the two were inextricably linked. From the windows of the main rooms the garden and park were no longer rigidly framed by allees and avenues leading to a statue or building. Instead a constant sweep of views was required, changing not just from one room to the next but even between the large sash windows newly installed in each grand room. Variety of experience was the watchword. Elegant and compact four-sided boxes were ideal to view a panorama of the whole landscape from the windows on three, or better still all four sides, like those that graced Brown's later parks at Benham Park, Berrington Hall and Claremont Estate. The ever-changing circuit within the house was mirrored subtly in the grounds where the circuit continually enticed the visitor to explore just that little bit further.

Brown made sure that in his landscape schemes the country house, whether he built it or not, was not merely a place to live in. It also became the focus of the whole landscape design, but it was vital to look out from the rooms as the views were carefully designed to be seen from the main rooms, often on the first floor (or *piano nobile*). Best of all was when he was in charge of the whole thing, house and grounds, giving him the greatest opportunity to design an artistic set piece for the owner. Berrington was one of his greatest opportunities to paint his landscape picture as a single work of art. Even though Holland designed the house, it is likely that Brown guided the siting and orientation of the house.

To understand Brown's landscape fully you have to see it from inside the house, which is the pivot in the landscape design. This is especially so at Claremont and Berrington, both four-sided boxes. At Claremont all four sides of the box relate to the landscape and the *piano nobile* circuit windows give an elevated view of the park and distant views over rolling Surrey. At Berrington the house on its high point enjoys spectacular views towards Wales. In both houses, as in others, colonnades and porticos were a classical way of both framing views out of the building and drawing the eye to it. The only other major ornamental building at Berrington is the detached triumphal arch gateway, by Holland, a major feature in the approach and surely heavily influenced by Brown. It is reminiscent of other arched gateways, including Earl Temple's Corinthian Arch at Stowe, put up in the 1760s to frame views between the mansion and the Buckingham Avenue approach. At Berrington both house and archway are built in the rich red sandstone distinctive of the area.

It was best if the offices (stables, kitchens, etc.) were banished to a distance so that the rational and symmetrical four-square effect of the house, if possible prominent on a rise, was fully visible and views from the rooms were undamaged by mere service buildings. Claremont is a marvellous example of this. Brown's house and offices were separated above ground in a sophisticated and successful way to show off the house in proud isolation, but linked by a tunnel. Tunnels were used occasionally at other places, such as Castle Coole, a Georgian country house in Northern Ireland. At Berrington the office courtyard is jammed up to the rear of the house, largely masking the north front. This was undoubtedly more practical, but it ruins the effect of all four sides of the house being part of the landscape.

The elegant elevations of these four-square houses were not only meant to be seen straight on in isolation. Oblique views from drives, public roads and walks gave an even richer effect of two sides of the composition at once, with the building glimpsed ever closer between park trees.

Brown's country houses built from scratch were largely carried out later in his career, with his architect son-in-law Henry Holland: Claremont (1771–4), Benham Park (1774–5), Cadland (1775–8) and Berrington (1778–81, attributed to Holland but surely heavily guided by Brown). Other houses built from scratch included those for Brown's long-time patron, Lord Coventry, whose Spring Hill (1763) was put up as a secondary residence to Croome Court. Fisherwick Hall, Staffordshire (1766–74) did not survive for long as it was demolished c.1818.

In 1781 Brown provided plans for 'An Intire New House' for Ickworth, Suffolk, for 100 guineas, where he had altered the grounds from 1768 for several years during the absence of a house. His house was never built, but instead the present spectacular drum was put up. Brown's proposed house was probably destined for this commanding position too, and it is likely that his previous landscaping work related to that site.

ABOVE | Claremont, Surrey, was Brown's first collaboration with his son-in-law, Henry Holland (1771–74). The client, Clive of India, and Brown both signed the drawings in the album of designs as part of the contract.

Elsewhere Brown remodelled existing houses. One of his earliest was in the 1750s at Croome, which was probably to Sanderson Miller's design. Externally the old house was unrecognisable though he invisibly retained the old internal walls as the skeleton. Some owners preferred a sleek but less drastic update. Perhaps they could not afford to knock down and build afresh or else they actually appreciated their ancient masonry and its evocation of equally venerable ancestry. Gloomy interiors were 'Georgianised' with elegant schemes featuring sash windows and airy new spacious wings. Brown did this sort of thing at Warwick Castle (1753–5), Burghley (1760s–70s), Brocklesby, Lincolnshire (1773) and Trentham, Staffordshire (1775–8 with Henry Holland). He enlarged Corsham Court (1761–4) including a fine picture gallery, remodelled by Redgrave, Suffolk c.1770, and altered Nuneham Courtenay in Oxfordshire (1781–2).

RIGHT | The interior design of the show rooms was important, but so was the view out to Brown's English Landcape Park which altered its appearance year-round. Berrington Hall was one of Brown's last landscape commissions, the house designed by Henry Holland and probably sited by Brown.

BELOW | Fashionable interior decor came as part of the design package offered by Brown. At Claremont this reception room featured imposing classical columns and elegant wall-mounted mirrors.

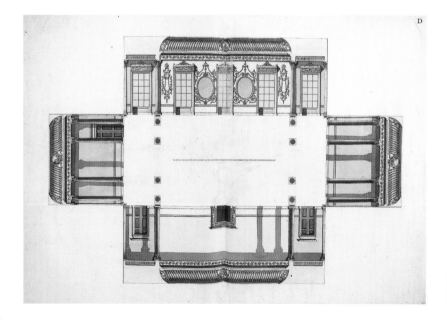

Horses and livestock: stables and farms

An increasing number of riding and carriage horses were kept by the mid-eighteenth century and so the need for adequate stabling became pressing. The idyllic pasture and hay meadows of Brown's parks were essential to feed and graze them, and at the same time the occupants manured them. The most opulent country-house stables had several ranges around a yard including a coach house, staff lodgings and storage for hay and feed. They were often as impressive in the landscape as the mansion.

Brown's imposing two-storey stable court at Burghley is in austere Gothic style alongside the great mansion ensemble. Three ranges of mellow local stone surround a large courtyard with a gateway in the wall across the fourth, north park side. The design he sent to Ireland for the stables at Slane Castle *c.*1770 is a less imposing ensemble, as the ranges are lower and enclose all four sides of the yard. The exterior is more ornamental than Burghley, echoing Gibbs's Gothic Temple at Stowe, newly built just as Brown arrived there in 1741. The whimsical decoration includes masks of inscrutable bearded men supporting the window sills. The interior of the yard is plainer, more utilitarian, but highly attractive. It is detached from the house, over 90m (100 yards) away and set in trees, in more typical Georgian fashion. The stable yard at Luton Hoo by Adam lies 230m (250 yards) from the house, and is surrounded by woodland, conveniently sited next to Brown's drives where they converge on the way to the house. At Burton Constable he

BELOW | Stables were often showpieces contributing to the landscape scene. Brown's Gothic stable block at Burghley, Lincolnshire, complements the Tudor house that he modified.

ABOVE | At Clandon Park,
Surrey, Brown's pair of lodges
announces the taste and wealth
of the owner once hidden
beyond the entrance. The house
was devastated by fire in April
2015, leaving its interior a shell
– though happily many of the
contents were saved.

designed the office courtyard in Gothic style (1772–3). Of around the same
date, at Fisherwick Hall in Staffordshire the coach house, stables and grooms'
quarters are in a roughly Z-shaped plan and classical in style, reminiscent
of Croome stables. His stable block at Clandon Park (*c.*1775), which stood
at some distance from the house, was demolished decades ago.

Dairies were fashionable and often doubled as decorative garden features.
Brown designed a dairy at Wynnstay, Denbighshire (1782) and in the pleasure
ground at Castle Ashby, a Kentian-style dairy (1760s) as an addition to the
home farm, seen from The Temple Menagerie in the park. Less ornamentally,
at Nuneham Courtenay House was the practical cattle tunnel in the north
park between his ox pens, through the ha-ha beneath Mason's picturesque
terrace, avoiding the pleasure ground.

Lodges and gates were important to monitor visitors and keep out
undesirables. Brown built the pair of elegant single-storey classical lodges
on the main road past the main entrance to Clandon Park (1776), on which
were hung early eighteenth-century iron gates (shown above). At Chilham
Castle in Kent (1777) his lodges have gone. He designed lodges for Blenheim,
at the Ditchley Gate, and for Packington in Warwickshire a grander pair with
an archway, but these remained unbuilt, as did the Gothic gateway and long
screen walls at Newton House (Dinefwr Castle).

Often parks incorporated the sites of lost villages. Many villages had, by
the 1750s, conveniently declined and gradually been removed by the land
owner. Wotton Underwood and Stowe villages had largely gone by the time
Brown arrived, leaving only the medieval churches, which were ignored in

the landscape design. Sometimes the owner objected to villagers living on his mansion doorstep and this led to the rebuilding of the village elsewhere, most notoriously at Nuneham Courtenay in the 1760s long before Brown arrived there. In Brown's own landscapes this happened several times. At Milton Abbas, Dorset, the town below the mansion, on the scale of Petworth or Corsham, was moved a mile or so away to a completely new site in a rather gloomy wooded valley. Brown's new, but Picturesque, thatched model village was completed with medievalising church and almshouses (*c.*1774–80) and enlivened the park scenery in the main approach past the lake. At Sledmere, East Yorkshire, the village was moved to a higher site in the 1770s. At Audley End Sir John Griffin Griffin moved a street of cottages out of the way of Brown's park.

Bridges

An elegant bridge, whether by him or another great architect, crowned a Brown landscape. These were in classical style generally and carried estate drives and paths over water, or else carried public roads that could not easily be moved. Sometimes they carried the park drive over a pleasure-ground

BELOW | This bridge at Compton Verney, Warwickshire, by Brown or Robert Adam, carries Brown's carriage drive to the house. One of Brown's signature London planes stands sentinel over it, in view from the house.

path. Others were sham bridges to disguise the break between two sheets of water by a dam. The most spectacular of park bridges was built some 50 years before Brown went near Blenheim, but he used Vanbrugh's huge erection to dominate his vast lake, created out of the trickling little River Glyme.

At Burghley his three-arched stone Lion Bridge (*c.* 1775) elegantly carries the main drive so that two sides of the house are clearly seen across the lake below from a carriage window or horseback. It is ornamented by pairs of lions on the parapet at either end. A similar bridge at Compton Verney (1770–2), guarded by pairs of sphinxes at either end, has the same effect so that two sides of the house are seen at once. The bridge carrying the public road over the Cam at Audley End is another in this group and again as placed carefully by Brown enjoys oblique views of the entrance front of the mansion. These bridges at Compton Verney and Audley End could be by Brown or Adam, who also worked there, as architects could all produce buildings with a similar look. In any case they are very similar to Brown's surviving design for the drive bridge at Ashburnham (1767). James Paine built similar bridges too. At Ashburnam Place, Sussex, *c.*1767 Brown designed a second, more ephemeral, timber bridge over the outlet of one of the lakes. His three-arched stone Scampston Bridge (*c.*1775) carried the main road from York.

The public road bridge at Compton Verney crosses the dam that cuts the sheet of water. It has five arches and a stone parapet and is more flat and workaday in outline than the elegantly curved three-arch bridge at the opposite end of the lake. A similar brick bridge carries one of the drives across the Cam at Audley End, facing Adam's pale stone bridge across the sheet of water. However, here the more ornamental bridge carries the public road rather than the park drive.

Covered bridges were occasionally used in pleasure grounds, opportunely placed for shelter. The Palladian Bridge at Scampston (1773–5) is white-painted plaster in classical style, with three narrow arches low-slung over the beck. It is a roofed pavilion supported by elegant columns, open to the widened beck to the south and sheltered by a wall to the north. It echoes in simpler form the stone Palladian Bridge at Stowe, itself copied from Wilton. Though the Palladian Bridge at Scampston cannot be seen from the Hall it is prominent from the park and parts of the garden. Robert Adam built something similarly gay and elegant at Audley End where the Cam left the pleasure ground.

The tunnel under Hampton Court Road linking Garrick's Villa and the riverside Shakespeare Temple was probably by Brown for his friend the

actor, theatre manager and playwright. Although principally for a path, it has a grotto-ish feel as the battered sides are faced with flint nodules, the arched tunnel vault is lined with slag and the riverside end has the opening of a picturesque grotto.

Sham bridges often disguised a change in level between water bodies, linking them visually into a single sheet. The one at Wotton Underwood is probably by Brown and is very similar to Kent's sham bridge at Stowe in the Elysian Fields. Later he designed a rustic sham bridge for Rothley, which was not built (shown below). At Chillington (before 1761) the upper lake water is impounded by the reddish stone, five-arch sham façade to carry a causeway between the two lakes. Cleverly disguising the change in level between two lakes at Burton Constable to make them seem a single sheet of water, he designed a real five-arched balustraded bridge carrying the drive (1778).

Cascades

Cascades were both functional and fun. As the outlet for the lake or river over a dam, they impersonated dramatic and noisy rocky rapids by grafting a layer of ragged rock on to the outer side of the dam. Brown built one in the late 1750s at Charlecote, near the mouth of the Wellesbourne Brook where it flows into the Avon, as part of his scheme raising, widening and serpentising the Brook. The cascade at Blenheim (recently rebuilt) is one of his most spectacular, where the water flows out of his Great Lake and returns to its real self as the little River Glyme. At Roche Abbey (c.1775), adjacent to Sandbeck, the cascade is of magnesian limestone, the blocks deeply

RIGHT | A sham bridge disguised the dam at the break between two sheets of water. Brown's rugged 1760s design for Rothley Lower Lake, Northumberland, would form the focus of the sheet of water but remained unbuilt.

coursed in tiers in a 2.7m (3-yard) drop so that the waters cascade noisily as a Picturesque landscape feature to enhance the setting of the Abbey ruins.

Boat houses

Boathouses were both functional and fun, to house the vessels for jolly boating times. The boathouse at Redgrave Park (c.1766–70) was an eye-catcher from Redgrave Hall (demolished). It was built of white brick and flint with stone dressings, of two storeys. At Coombe Abbey the boathouse attributed to Brown (1770s) stands on the south side of The Pool. Marked on a plan of 1778, it is of red brick and single storey, open ended to The Pool with an entrance door opposite.

Brown's boathouse at Petworth is one of the most imposing and unusual. It is to be seen across the water and also provides a platform from which to view the main lake and house and extensive Sussex views. Built c.1756 the stone building is set into an artificial grassed earth bank and has the air of a military emplacement. The main façade above the water has two arches at water level with above these a massive keystone with a Neptune sculpture probably salvaged from the Fount House of 1694. On top the viewing platform has a seat from which to take in the magnificent views. The whole structure is supported by massive flanking walls.

Garden buildings

Gardens and parks were for fun, exercise and contemplation, and playful buildings were at the heart of this. Some of Brown's landscapes are sprinkled with garden buildings both by him and others, such as Croome, while at the contemporary Petworth they are less numerous. At still others they are almost absent from his design, with the mansion as the sole ornamental garden building. Berrington has the great triumphal arch gateway (by Holland) and the rare semicircular kitchen garden. Ashridge's Golden Valley has no Brownian park buildings at all.

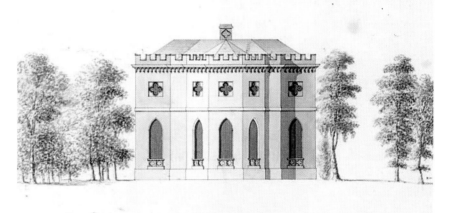

Brown's garden buildings were of varying sizes and types, in Gothic, classical and other quirky styles. At Burghley House the little Gothic summerhouse in the pleasure ground overlooking the lake is based on one of the pair of banqueting houses at the early seventeenth-century Chipping Campden House, Gloucestershire. As engaging, still in Gothic, is the two-storey Corsham Court Bath House (1760s). It is approached via a gloomy path to the rear, to give a surprise view of the pleasure grounds from the dressing room above the ground-floor bath, and in turn forms a garden feature. The plainer rectangular Banqueting House at Old Wardour is credited to him, standing below the late medieval Wardour Castle ruin commanding views back up to the castle as well as over the pond in the park

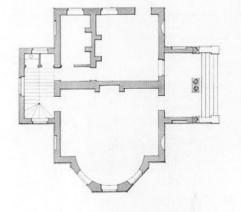

and beyond to the Georgian mansion. Brown designed an unbuilt Gothic banqueting house as the focus for Rothley Lake, Northumberland. The tall, three-storey classical Owl House in the walled kitchen garden at Wallington is believed to be by him as is the similar banqueting house at Talacre, Flintshire, a close relation in stone in the walled garden there. A design for a similar building and garden wall has turned up in the Earl of Bute's papers at

ABOVE | Brown's Banqueting House, Rothley Lower Lake, Northumberland (1760s) was one of a suite of buildings he proposed around the lake including a sham castle and sham bridge.

Mount Stuart in Scotland. The whimsical little Shell House at Hatfield Forest was not by Brown it seems, but was the focal building on the shores of his lake-scape.

Monumental Roman columns were purely ornamental, as a statement of the owner's wealth and power. Often a narrow spiral stair allowed the intrepid up to a perilous viewing platform or belvedere perched at the top to gaze over the owner's estate lands. Brown's first such monument was the mighty Cobham Monument (1747–8) at Stowe, built for Lady Cobham as an eye-catcher for the Elysian Fields to commemorate her husband. It was possibly designed by James Gibbs but Brown at least oversaw its erection. Reminiscent in scale of the Duke of Marlborough's Column of Victory in the park at Blenheim, the 30.5m (100ft) high fluted stone column at Stowe supports a statue of Lord Cobham on a viewing belvedere on one of the high points of the estate. Both columns can be seen from many parts of their respective park, pleasure ground and distant countryside. At Burton Pynsent, Somerset, Brown designed The Column for his close friend, prime minster

BELOW | Georgians loved rotundas in their gardens. Redolent of Roman Italy, like this example at Croome, Worcestershire, which rests in a shrubbery walk, commanding the scene over half Brown's park.

Lord Chatham (Pitt the Elder). The pillar was put up *c*.1765, the cupola topped by a large urn.

Brown offered to help in the construction of the column at Gibside, Tyne and Wear. He wrote: '…if you pleas to send me a rough Sketch of it, with the Weight of a Cubik Foot of The Stone I will put you in the Way That you will be Sure to have your Building Stand', adding that the scaffolding was of the greatest importance after the foundations. His letter ended: 'If I can be the least useful to you I beg you May Command me because I Should have a Double pleasure in it your Situation being My Native Country.' His offer was not taken up, but the owner, Bowes, ensured his column was taller and with a larger statue than that at Stowe.

Brown's Gothic parish church (1758–63) at Croome replaced the old medieval building on a new site. High up on a ridge, it stands in imposing isolation across the park from the drives and house. In contrast the family chapel at Compton Verney (1776–8) is a classical box, tucked away behind the house next to the kitchen garden, though one of the drives goes right past it.

Ornamental greenhouses in the garden or pleasure ground were for tender exotic 'greens' (evergreens) and flowering plants, rather than large-scale produce. They usually faced south for maximum warmth and light. Brown's greenhouse design for Ashburnham Place has five bays in a rhythmic classical style with soothing round-headed arches, and he was paid £600 in 1777 'on account of the Greenhouse'. His Ashburnham design is almost identical to the lost Hot House at Compton Verney, which was guarded by four sphinxes on the plinth outside and also to the lost greenhouse at Stoke Place, Buckinghamshire. At Croome his Hot House, the guide book informed visitors, grew such a vast variety of plants that 'the Stranger might almost fancy himself transported, at once, if that were possible, into the eastern and western world. For here, he will see, assembled, and growing luxuriantly together, the palms, the cinnamon, the laurus-cassia of the former, and the pimentos, plantains, coffee, and the bread-fruit tree of the latter'. Brown's Orangery at Burghley is a grand beast, much longer, and in busy Gothic, with large sash windows, topped by a crenellated parapet and onion-domed turrets to fit in with the style of the great house. These usually overlooked their own little gardens or terraces in which some of the tubbed 'greens' could be displayed in summer.

At Nuneham, he recommended a Gothic Ruin to stand on a distant pleasure ground eminence visible from the house, at the end of what was called Brown's Walk overlooking the Thames. This was not built, but the idea of a

venerable structure on the site was implemented a little later. When the 1617 Carfax Conduit that housed the main Oxford city water source, was being moved, it was rebuilt on the site in 1786. It is still an eye-catcher in Brown's landscape and would have pleased him for it is of a similar early Stuart period to the styles he used for the Corsham Bath House and Burghley Summerhouse.

Brown could turn his hand to all sorts of buildings needed to enliven the landscape. At Ashburnham Place it is fascinating to compare his designs of *c*.1767 for a suite of buildings with the positions he intended for them on his plan of alterations to the park and gardens. As well as the greenhouse, he designed alterations to offices next to the house, two new bridges and an imposing gateway. A classical temple, distant across the lake, is probably also his, and very useful to shelter in during a shower. On his plan though he specified instead a larger Gothic building, 'to be put at the back of the shrubbery'. Even so, the temple catches the eye in the morning as the distant gothick one at Temple Newsam, Leeds, does in the evening. In the 1770s he designed another group, of around seven buildings, for Coombe Abbey.

The Roman rotunda is ornamental in the landscape scenes, usually imbued with an allegorical theme to guide the viewer's thoughts. More practically, it offers shelter and a place to take refreshment and to frame panoramic views. It often housed a statue of Venus or another mythical figure such as Hercules. The graceful cylindrical confection had a dome for a lid. Sometimes the sides were open and bristling with columns, or else enclosed by walls as a garden room. The Bath stone Rotunda at Croome (1753) is one of Brown's early garden buildings and commands the scene of half of the park. A solid classical drum, at the end of the Home Shrubbery walk past the kitchen garden, it stands proudly on an eminence overlooking the park and surrounding countryside to the Malverns and Cotswolds.

A great contrast to Croome's rather masculine rotunda, is the Garden House, Great Saxham Hall in Suffolk, perhaps by Brown who supervised the landscaping. This lightweight and ephemeral stucco folly, open to the sides, was perhaps a Temple of Dido. In elegant Strawberry Hill Gothic style, its domed roof was carried by slender clustered columns and pointed arches, making it a very feminine building. His Petworth pleasure ground acquired a standard open classical rotunda a few years after he had finished there, prominent above a steep bank above the London Road.

GLOOMY GROTTOES

The point of a grotto on the garden circuit was purely emotional, to provoke great heights and depths of feeling. The essence of the grotto contrasted gloomy foreboding, pleasurable surprise and, with luck, a terrific sparkle never forgotten.

The idea originated in classical Greece and Rome as the shrine to the spirit of a spring, usually a nubile nymph or bearded river god. Some had resident deities as scantily clad and perpetually wetted statues. In the Georgian garden many were enthusiastically created with great imagination, and often expense. The interior was best found as a surprise, so the approach was artfully concealed in the pleasure ground in a natural hillside or behind banks of imported earth planted with evergreen shrubs, framing a dark and terrifying entrance. 'Grottish' and 'grotesque' described the desired effect.

Brown's Clandon grotto (*c.*1781) is a damp, flinty Surrey cave and bath house. Its entrance arches open to the garden and house. It leads back 5.5m (6 yards) into the hill with a statue of the Three Graces inside. A shallow stone bath sunk into the floor at the back should be fed by a trickle of water, home of the resident water nymph. The one at Croome is in a flat pleasure ground and the mounded earthen and rocky surrounds trying to set it into the landscape are entirely artificial. The walls of its little caves are bursting with mineral incrustations and ammonites, overlooking a backwater of Brown's nearby park river meant to emulate the Severn. When it was later altered an elegant Coade stone statue was added, supposedly of Sabrina, the seductively reclining goddess of the River Severn.

ABOVE | Brown's frothy summerhouse in the pleasure ground at Burghley overlooks the lake and park beyond.

Beastly buildings

Keeping rare and exotic animals was popular in parks and pleasure grounds, usually in a menagerie with pens at the back. Of Brown's park buildings, one of the most impressive was the Gothic Park Farm menagerie at Blenheim (1760s), carefully screened with trees. John Byng visiting in 1787 noted the exotics that the Duke kept included 'two beautiful deer call'd blue cow deer, from the East Indies; a remarkably fine Spanish ass, [from whom all the fine mules who work in the park are descended]; and two moose deer from America, the oddest shapen and ugliest animals I ever saw ...'. Another occupant was a tiger the Duke was sent by Clive of India.

The austere classical menagerie at Coombe Abbey was the most poetic of a group of seven park buildings in the Brown landscape scheme of the 1770s, including lodges, boat-house and Gothic kennels either by Brown, or perhaps Henry Holland. The Menagerie's distinctive hexagonal domed tower was inspired by Louis XIV's Royal Menagerie at Versailles. On a high point at the far end of the park, it catches the eye in long views over the lake.

The elegant Temple Menagerie at Castle Ashby (1761) is more sophisticated in its Neo-classical design than Brown's Dairy there, and some think it is by Robert Adam. It housed exotic and home-grown birds and animals, and some 700 were listed in an account book. The livestock lived in pens behind the elegant curved, semicircular portico, seen from the house across a sweeping lake.

BELOW | A grotto was the most whimsical of garden buildings, the interior often decorated with colourful minerals and shells. At Croome, Worcestershire, a statue of the river goddess Sabrina was added.

Kitchen gardens

The kitchen garden was the heart of every country-house estate. It fed not just the family and household staff but often provided for the family town house too. It was laid out formally with paths and beds in quadrants to maximise production and efficiency, never succumbing to the serpentine lines that pervaded the rest of the estate. Brown had done perhaps fifty walled gardens by 1760 and dozens more followed.

Brown was an enthusiastic kitchen gardener and for this he and his like were derided by his rival William Chambers as 'well skilled in the culture of salads, but little acquainted with the principles of ornamental gardening'. Brown designed many kitchen gardens, but the designs for the layouts do not seem to be distinctive, following convention and allowing the resident head gardener to dictate how they were used. Before his time the kitchen garden was often part of the group of structures around the house. As the century progressed, in order to allow the house to stand free of other structures, it was often pushed well away to a remote corner of the park if the will and means of the owner allowed.

A southerly aspect was best. The walls were prized not just for shelter for the interior beds but also to support fruit trees and glasshouses, offering precious additional warmth and shelter. Brick was the best available material as it warmed up quickly in spring. Often in an area of stone building material this is used for the outer face, with expensive imported brick for the inner skin. Sometimes walls were heated by flues from a fireplace to force fruit trees to blossom earlier. This was a bit of a black art and not very reliable to maintain the required constant gentle heat.

The area around the outside, the slips, was valuable for the additional shelter the walls offered, and was often cultivated. Glasshouses were commonly built against south-facing walls. The head gardener's house was often set into a wall. Potting sheds, fruit stores, boilers and other lesser structures stood on the dank far side of the north wall where valuable sunshine never penetrated.

Many kitchen gardens are difficult to attribute firmly to Brown's hand. Where a whole park is his and a new kitchen garden appeared, then he is almost certainly the author, but possibly with alterations by others. The walled gardens associated with him have various shapes. The straightforward, conventional one at Basildon (1778) lies in the valley some 274m (300 yards) from the house. It is brick-walled, rectangular and encloses 3½ acres, the design for which he charged 50 guineas (quite a sum). This is his only recorded work in Basildon Park.

The vast rectangular kitchen garden at Ashburnham Place, East Sussex measures some 165 x 78m (180 x 85 yards). It is placed on a ridge and surrounded by 4.3m (14ft) high walls of expensive red brick with the expanse of red masonry broken up by burnt grey headers. The rest of the estate buildings used the cheaper local Wealden stone. Brown sheltered it further with a shrubbery walk around the outside, like that at Croome, and both stand next to the stables and quite close to the house. The layout at Ashburnham was the traditional cruciform pattern of paths surrounded by a circuit path below the walls and it has the usual ornamental stone dipping pool. The walled Melon Ground lay adjacent to the east side, including 'stoves' or hot houses, an orchard to the west, and against the cold dark outer side of the north wall were the working sheds.

At Nuneham Courtenay a similar 3-acre kitchen garden remains largely as Brown showed on his plan of 1779. It stands next to the stables out in the park. The gardener's house is built into the west wall and at the main entrance in the east wall an ornamental gateway is flanked by eighteenth-century iron gates with an elaborate scrolled overthrow.

Not all kitchen gardens were traditional rectangles. A few were enclosed with more than four walls to give maximum exposure to precious warming south-facing sunlight. Some had cross walls for further shelter and room to train fruit trees. The irregular L-shaped ornamental Walled Garden for Sir Walter Calverley

Blackett at Wallington is probably Brown's (c.1766). Into the north side is built the Owl House, an elevated garden room in expensive brick, overlooking the sloping brick-walled kitchen garden below to the park beyond and James Paine's elegant road bridge. On the roof perches the eponymous stone owl, the Calverley family crest. A similar, but stone, building at Talacre in Wales is probably Brown's too, and a design for a similar building survives in Lord Bute's archive at Mount Stuart.

A pentagonal kitchen garden was part of his layout at Brocklesby Park near Grimsby in 1771. Estate accounts confirm that building the walls of the 5-acre garden began in 1773 and took three years to complete. A head gardener's cottage was attached, with a 'slip garden' in the surrounding area outside the walls, and a gardeners' yard with glasshouses to the north including a fine vinery. This ensemble still largely survives.

Octagonal kitchen gardens were expensive and rare, but they helped to trap still more effectively the warming rays of the sun as it appeared at various angles and heights at different times of year. Sledmere in the rolling Yorkshire Wolds is probably part of Brown's late 1770s park scheme. It was built in the mid-1780s, measuring some 91 x 82m (100 x 90 yards) and covering over 2 acres. Still more impressive is his octagonal kitchen garden at Luton Hoo (late 1760s), again part of a scheme for the whole park. It is a vast brick-walled sun trap, over 457m (500 yards) in circumference, enclosing some 5 acres. Sited on a plateau at the high point of the park, it, like the one at Ashburnham, faces south-east to obtain maximum morning sun. A 137m (150-yard) long central cross wall increases the great expanse of warm wall space still further. In total Lord Bute set aside 10 acres, including the slips outside. This also contained Lord Bute's renowned botanical garden and great conservatory, which might have been by Brown or Adam.

Horseshoe-shaped kitchen gardens are very rare indeed, because they took much skill and cost to build. A curved south-facing wall led to the cross wall across the south side. The curved wall was believed to improve air circulation with fewer hideyholes for pests. Opinions were not all positive. Thomas Hitt in his *Treatise of Fruit Trees* wrote in 1757 that curved brick walls generated more heat than straight walls, but that this advantage was outweighed by strong winds which, bouncing from side to side, damaged tender shoots. Brown's curved kitchen garden wall at Berrington (*c*.1780) is south-facing. Its expensive red brick entirely ignores the abundant local red sandstone which was used for Holland's boxy house. The sweeping curve is 73m (80 yards) across its widest point, but is obscured by lean-to cattle byres, as it has been for many years a farmyard.

By contrast Wynnstay's horseshoe-shaped kitchen garden, perhaps also by Brown, is today spectacularly reopened, in one of the largest and most important eighteenth-century landscape parks in Wales. At some 128 (140 yards) across at its widest point, the garden shows off the scale in an impressive formal sweep. The unusual masonry of its 3.6m (12ft) high red brick wall is varied in different bandings, with stone copings. The wall is remarkable for being unbuttressed, its strength derived from the curved line. The central section is a cavity wall with heating flues for circulating warm air from a stove through vents in the brickwork to improve growing and ripening fruit.

Ice houses

Georgian ice houses were purely functional and not for show, quietly storing ice for use in the house. To be kept as cool as possible, ideally they sank into a north-facing slope, embowered in evergreens such as yew. For added insulation the domed top of the main chamber was covered in earth and planted with evergreen shrubs. Some domes stood proud with a thatched roof over the conical main chamber and the approach tunnel. Brown's recently re-thatched ice house at Compton Verney is in an ornamental wood near the lake, convenient for harvesting ice in winter. The one at Croome is very similar, but is high on a ridge in a wooded pleasure ground well away from the source of ice in the lake. A 6ft (2 yard) long tunnel forms an air lock to keep the chamber from warming up. Others attributed to him include those at Ashridge, Milton Abbey and Tong Castle, and numerous others are likely his.

BELOW | Brown's ice house at Compton Verney, Warwickshire; its ovoid brick chamber was buried and thatched to keep the precious ice from melting.

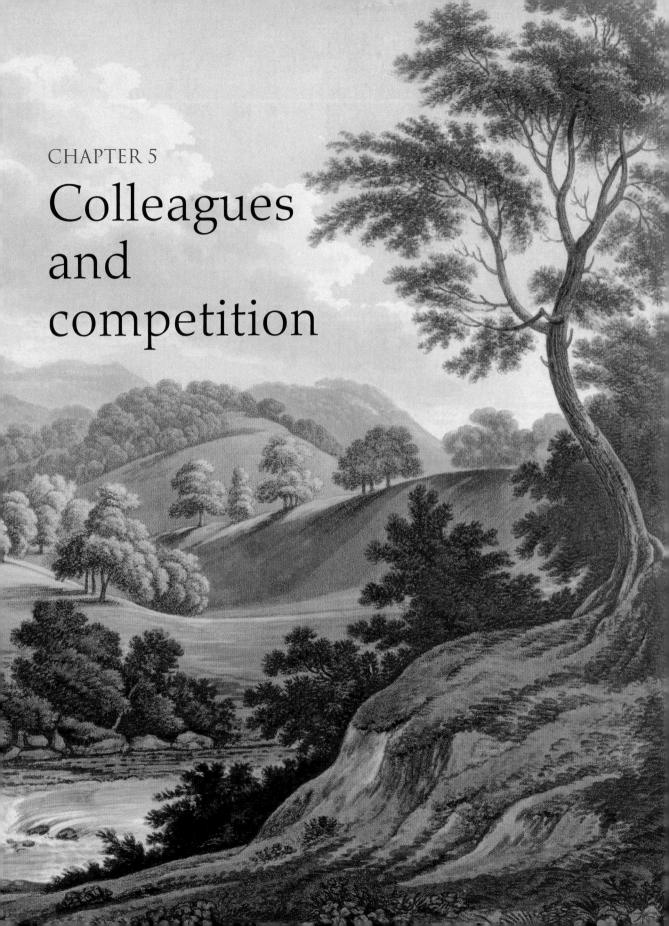

CHAPTER 5

Colleagues
and
competition

The home and away teams

Brown was the star of a group of able landscapers, both amateur and professional, at the heart of the English Landscape Garden. He was streets ahead of the competition thanks to his winning combination of artistry, technical expertise, business acumen and easy manner, and an unequalled client list. His portfolio of some 250 or more sites could not be rivalled. Britain's elite landscape owners were begging him to go and see them and advise. Even so, he was not the only landscaper on the block. Around him plenty of others made a good living out of the wealth of landowners who were driven to follow the English landscape fashion. This chapter looks at the 'home' and 'away' teams: Brown's associates and rivals.

Some of his competitors began on Brown's 'home' team, coming and going as he needed them, launching out into their own independent careers when they felt the time was right. Others, the rival 'away' team, had entirely independent careers. Naturally, as his career progressed his rivals and protégés increasingly filled the gaps he left in the market, particularly Thomas White and Nathaniel Richmond from his 'home' team, and William Emes and Richard Woods who led the 'away' team. It seems they offered a cheaper service, which may have been a major consideration for some clients. Some picked up prestigious jobs for the aristocracy, but none equalled the extent or glory of Brown's clientele or countrywide coverage.

The 'home' team – Brown's staff

Brown may have been an artistic genius and astute businessman, but he could not sustain this vast number of commissions without a reliable and extensive team to execute his vision. His foremen, surveyors and draughtsmen are the unsung heroes of his story. He did not take on pupils to train, like architects did, but employed men who were already

PREVIOUS PAGE | Hafod, near Aberystwyth, is in the more rugged and sublimely scary Picturesque style that succeeded Brown's work.

BELOW | At Kedleston Hall, Derbyshire, one of the greatest Georgian architects, Robert Adam, made his only major foray into landscape design. His pleasure-ground walk full of sinuous curves was carried out in simplified form (*Plan for Kedleston Pleasure Ground*, Robert Adam, c.1760).

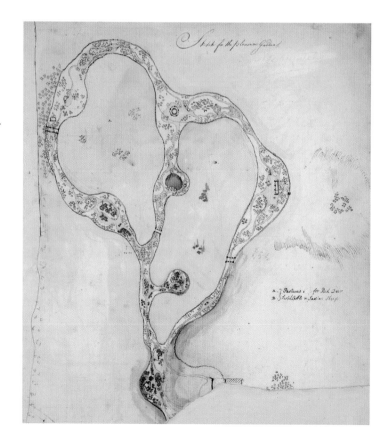

competent. It was tricky enough to keep his clients happy without novice staff making the mistakes of inexperience. Once he had seen competent men in action he knew he could rely on them and gave them unparalleled opportunities to prove themselves. A number set out on their own after making a name for themselves with Brown. This did not trouble him unduly, as he was always more than busy enough himself. Information about his staff is only found in bits and pieces, gleaned from many sources.

BACK-UP: THE OFFICE TEAM

By the time he moved to Hampton Court in 1764 Brown needed an office team to support his busy practice. He leased a yard and set up an office. He took on two trained surveyors, Samuel Lapidge and Jonathan Spyers, who slogged out to the sites either with him or after he visited and sometimes spent weeks surveying. They returned to the office to draft surveys and proposal plans. Brown drew up some plans, but many are by the more polished hands of Lapidge and Spyers, who were his closest and longest-standing colleagues and stayed with him until his death.

Lapidge (d.1806) from Hampton had the closer relationship with Brown. He came the nearest to being his assistant, and Brown made him executor of his will. He completed the outstanding schemes after Brown's death in 1783 and noted final payments by creditors in Brown's account book. He was the father of Edward Lapidge, the architect of Kingston Bridge in 1825 and the new church at Hampton in 1830. Brown was one of his godfathers.

Spyers (*d*.1798), from nearby Twickenham, was also a nurseryman. He carried out much of the survey work from 1764, replacing William Donn and Thomas White who carried out earlier surveys. He was a talented watercolour draughtsman who produced many landscape scenes mainly of Hampton Court and Bushy Park while Brown was in charge. The Anglophile Russian empress Catherine the Great bought 150 of these in the early 1780s. She paid the huge sum of 1,000 roubles for her collection, which remains in The Hermitage in St Petersburg (in comparison, laying out the vast park around the English Palace in the 1780s cost 10,000 roubles). These scenes are a remarkable record of how the gardens looked under Brown's management. While Spyers was a competent landscape painter, the figures who populate and enliven the views are amusingly slender, almost stick people. The Hermitage collection also includes designs for garden buildings, and landscape and garden views elsewhere, possibly for unexecuted schemes.

FOREMEN

Competent foremen were essential to fulfilling Brown's vision on the ground, able to manage a large body of workmen and keep the work rate up. Several names crop up time and again in his account books and in the papers of the estates they worked at. His site foremen were also often skilled surveyors, such as Cornelius Griffin who surveyed Copped Hall, Essex, probably before he went to Alnwick in 1769.

Jonathan Midgley worked with Brown for nearly 20 years from 1760, including as foreman at Charlecote and Castle Ashby. He also worked for other clients independently. He was paid directly by the client at Ashburnham from 1776–81, more than £8,600 in total, when Brown was separately paid £2,000.

The Scot Michael Milliken (*d*.1800) worked for Brown at Chatsworth from 1760. Here, as an outsider, he deftly and tactfully managed a team of estate workers, implementing Brown's design and keeping the estate managers happy too. In 1765 Brown brought him to Kew to carry out the landscaping works at Richmond Gardens for the king, where he stayed as gardener for 35 years. Brown envisaged that Milliken would be carrying out a 'great and lasting worke' where he would be 'known to his Majesty and other Great Men'. He quietly raised Milliken's wages more than he expected, and more than the master had paid anyone else, on the understanding that it was a secret not even Lapidge would know of, or 'it would raise a murmuring amongst his other men'. On Brown's death George III is said to have remarked 'Now Mellicant, you and I can do here [Kew] what we please.'

Benjamin Read was the principal water engineer in the 'home' team. He worked at two of the most prestigious and extensive schemes: at Croome (1760–5, this bit costing some £4,000) and Blenheim (1760s). He also worked at the very watery Wotton Underwood for spells during the 1750s and 1760s, with large payments in the 1750s. Lord Coventry asked Brown for Read to return to Croome in 1772 when his 'River Severn' sprang a leak due to tree roots in the banks, Read being a 'Man of Practice' as the Earl called him. William Ireland possibly started out at Wallington, Northumberland. After this he was working for Brown 1768–83, on jobs at Burghley, Luton Hoo, Stapleford and Trentham. In the 1780s he worked for Lapidge. Alexander Knox, perhaps a Scot, worked at lesser schemes, at North Stoneham and Branches, Essex. Cornelius Griffin worked at Redgrave, Maiden Early and Alnwick; Andrew Gardiner at Sandbeck and North Stoneham; George Bowstreed at Southill Park, Bedfordshire and Wimbledon; Cornelius Dickinson at Harewood and Sherborne.

BELOW | Brown's foremen translated his vision to the ground. At Alnwick Castle, Northumberland, Thomas Biesley managed a team of dozens of men in the 1770s then stayed for good, becoming Superintendent of Parks and Rides.

An odd situation occurred at Alnwick Castle. Brown sent a succession of foremen who managed large teams alongside those of the Duke's own man, Thomas Call. Side by side, these two teams landscaped the vast parks and pleasure grounds over decades from the 1760s. This must have been tricky to accomplish alongside the local staff, particularly to keep Call on side, who was well established as the top man in the parks and was highly respected on design by the Duke of Northumberland. Firstly Cornelius Griffin went in 1769, but having been taken ill in the summer of 1772, he died in harness. Brown, who was himself ill at this time, arranged for a replacement, and sent Thomas Robson who had been part of the team at their London property, Syon. Robson was soon replaced by Thomas Biesley who managed a team of dozens of men over the following years.

Biesley, despite being a southern outsider, was clearly happy at Alnwick for he spent 40 years there, first as Brown's foreman, then as the Keeper of Parks and Pleasure Grounds. He continued in post until his death in 1814, aged 82.

Adam Mickle senior was the gardener at Badminton, Gloucestershire, where he worked from 1743–57, with William Kent in the 1740s, and then with Brown when he was there early in his freelance career in 1752. It seems that only Brown's walled garden was executed, although plans survive for other schemes. Mickle left Badminton and was employed by Brown in 1757. He spent 20 or so years with him, including working on Sandbeck and Roche Abbey, then in 1779 set up on his own, shortly before Brown died.

Brown did not work closely with an architect for more than 20 years after he set up on his own, managing the building design himself as required. Eventually he began to work with Henry Holland, architect and son of the builder Brown had worked with when he first went out on his own. The younger Henry joined Brown in 1771 in an informal partnership that lasted successfully until Brown's death in 1783. Holland started in this career with Brown by building the new house for Clive of India at Claremont. In 1773, while they were working on Claremont, he married Brown's daughter Bridget and as a dowry Brown made over the large sum of £5,000 in consolidated stock.

Holland must have inspired considerable confidence in Brown. He took on most of Brown's architectural commissions and benefited from his father-in-law's large and influential clientele to set up his career, in the absence of professional pupillage and foreign travel. Their last commission was Berrington Hall in a fine *tour de force*, with the house crowning Brown's landscape park and embracing the wider Herefordshire countryside.

BELOW | Holland's massive gateway at Berrington Hall, Herefordshire, is in the same austere style of his red sandstone house. Brown probably sited both, for maximum effect in his park.

The 'away' team – the competition

Brown's English Landscape style was not unique, but he was the most prolific and renowned in the field. Various foremen worked for him, 20 or more, and some naturally moved on to work independently while plenty of others were in competition with him. Repton blamed inept imitators for the subsequent criticism of Brown's style by the Picturesque men, who wanted everything much more rugged, mouldering and less smooth. The 'away' team divided into two parts: gentlemen, who had the means to design their own grounds or the talent to do so for others in an unpaid capacity; and players, men without social connections or large landed incomes, who needed to make a living.

GENTLEMEN

Amongst the professionals were gifted amateurs, landowners who had the vision and understanding of their properties to lay out inspiring and

engaging landscapes on a great scale. These were the most able of men, their artistry often more gifted than Brown's paid rivals, with the extensive means needed to execute their vision. Lord Cobham at Stowe was one of the greatest, although he employed the best designers of the day to execute his vision. Rich banker Henry Hoare laid out a Virgilian route around his lakes at Stourhead on the Wiltshire/Dorset border, spilling out into the vast wider wooded landscape and punctuating the views with large, expensive buildings. The Hon. Charles Hamilton at Painshill, Surrey, was a cash-strapped younger son of aristocracy who laid out his great garden and populated it with garden buildings with panache. On a shoestring the gentleman poet

William Shenstone retreated in 1744 to The Leasowes, Staffordshire, turning the estate into a landscape garden, or *ferme ornée*. This, said Dr Johnson, 'he did with such judgement and such fancy as made his little domain the envy of the great and gained the admiration of the skilful: a place to be visited by travellers, and copied by designers'. As well as a wide variety of root houses, seats, urns and cascades, he used inscriptions from ancient poets to interpret and enliven the circuit. Apparently he coined the phrase 'landskip-gardening'.

All of these became acclaimed places on the tourist route, and influential for those keen to emulate their Arcadian successes. Many other owners, such as Lord Scarsdale at Kedleston, had a considerable influence on their final park layout even when they employed professional designers.

Alongside the owner-amateurs were gentlemen amateur designers who advised their circle. Sanderson Miller (1716–80) was one such, also an owner, mostly an architect but with a strong feel for landscape design. He began in the mid-1740s with his own modest estate at Radway in Warwickshire, building an octagonal Gothic tower nearby on a promontory at Edgehill. This was the first of his efforts, until around 1760, to establish medieval resonances in landscapes, particularly using fake Gothic ruins. With his society connections he offered significant advice on buildings and grounds, at over 20 places centred on Warwickshire and Oxfordshire, including Wroxton, Oxfordshire, Hagley in Worcestershire, Lacock in Wiltshire, Ingestre Hall in Staffordshire, and Wimpole in Cambridgeshire. His historic mock-ups were so convincing that Horace Walpole admitted that the 'medieval' castle at Hagley seemed to have 'the true rust of the Barons' war.' Miller was a great promoter of Brown from his earliest independent days, starting out in 1749, and introduced him to many of his wide, wealthy circle.

Sir Roger Newdigate at Arbury Hall, Warwickshire was another Midland owner and amateur architect with landscape leanings, part of the Sanderson Miller circle, who advised friends and family. He too was an early exponent of the Gothic revival in architecture. He advised his brother-in law John Conyers on the grounds at Copped Hall, Essex when he was rebuilding his house in the 1740s–50s, including where to site the classical house to greatest effect, on the crest of the ridge in the park.

PLAYERS

The players were those men who needed to make a living because they came from a lower social strata of slender means. They mostly started out as gardeners, surveyors, improvers and nurserymen, all related disciplines. Few were as artistically inspired as Brown or the best of the gentlemen landowners, but they were capable and perhaps more reliable in their attendance than Brown, and cheaper to employ. The most prolific had moments of inspiration, such as lakes by William Emes at Hawkstone and Adam Mickle at Tredegar, and Richard Woods's Great Terrace Walk at Wardour Castle, but in general they were not regarded by their contemporaries as highly as Brown, whose publicity machine insisted that he was 'the face' of the landscape park, and those who employed him liked to think that they only employed the best.

BELOW | Thomas Wright was an eccentric architect and landscaper, known as the 'Wizard of Durham'. He designed the rugged Codger Fort at Wallington, Northumberland, as an eyecatcher, high on a moor overlooking Brown's Rothley Lakes.

Thomas Wright (1711–86), known as the Wizard of Durham, was not as privileged as the gentlemen amateurs, but like them was seldom paid for his designs it seems. He was not hugely influential or productive but managed to build a client list that was impressive. An astronomer, designer of garden buildings and landscape gardener, he, like Brown, was a self-made man from yeoman stock, and from the same remote part of England. Unlike Brown, who fitted in wherever he landed, Wright was an odd, eccentric man, but even so he was embraced and widely passed around in high society to teach mathematics and astronomy.

Living on the fringes of high society, his portfolio was much smaller than Brown, but he contributed to at least 15 gardens, many for movers and shakers including various peers. His style was similar to that of William Kent and he designed many garden buildings including rustic grottoes, some quite eccentric. He was taken up by the Earl of Pembroke in 1735, then by the Duke and Duchess of Kent at Wrest Park, Bedfordshire, as a teacher for themselves and their children. He was renowned for the famous river and terrace at Oatlands, Surrey, for Lord Lincoln. He worked at Wallington, Northumberland, for Sir Walter Blackett where he designed the miniature Codgers Fort overlooking Brown's Rothley Lakes, and at several gardens in Ireland including Dundalk, Tullymore and Belvedere. His most notable landscape work was at Badminton, Gloucestershire, close to Bath, in the 1750s for the Duke of Beaufort, where he produced a fussy, over-wriggly design for the woodland garden, and numerous structures including a grotto. He published his two volumes of *Universal Architecture* with engaging designs for arbours and grottoes in 1755 and 1758.

Thomas White (1739–1811) was a Shropshire man, a surveyor, whose patch was northern England and Scotland. He advised at well over 100 estates on planting and landscaping, beginning in Yorkshire and the north of England and latterly in Scotland. He started out as foreman for Brown including at Temple Newsam, Yorkshire, 1762–5, and left Brown to go to nearby Harewood as a surveyor in his own right. Coming from the Brown team, he was of similar stamp, being industrious and willing to travel great distances. His early commissions in Yorkshire led to his first Scottish commission in 1770. All his new jobs after about 1787 were in Scotland, including Scone Palace, which is well documented in the 1780s. Like his competitors, many of his jobs stretched over a long period, such as Belle Isle on Windermere, Cumbria (1783–96), which included plantations on the mountain sides above the lake. He may also have landscaped the renowned Claife Station, a tourist viewing station on a rock overlooking Belle Isle, reached by a winding path cut into the rock above the landing stage. Some plans remained unexecuted and others were adapted by the owner. When he died in 1811, his son Thomas continued the practice until at least 1820. White Senior was said to be an innovator, introducing many new improvements, which were much admired. He received medals for his tree planting achievements from the Royal Society of Arts.

William Emes (1729/30–1803) was a rival to Brown in the Midlands and Wales, with at least ninety commissions. He had no personal connection with Brown and he even replaced him at Eaton Hall in Cheshire for Earl Grosvenor in 1763 after the peer had spent at least £800 on Brown. At some places he executed Brown's suggestions, including Tixall in 1770, and at Ingestre he implemented them partially, after Brown had gone. It was common for an owner to obtain suggestions from a couple of designers, or call in a second designer if what the first was doing was not to the owner's liking.

A native of Derbyshire, Emes started out in the 1750s at Kedleston for Lord Curzon, becoming head gardener in 1756 aged 27. In the same way that the Grecian Valley was Brown's major contribution to the developing landscape at Stowe before he set out on his own, so the Upper Lake at Kedleston was the major project that Emes learnt on (his lake held water however, where Brown's Grecian Valley never did). He overlapped with Robert Adam at Kedleston. Adam, although principally rebuilding the mansion and designing park buildings, very unusually produced a complex plan for a pleasure-ground walk round part of the park in 1759, which was executed in simplified form. This was Adam's only major venture into landscape design and though the plan is his, it was probably inspired by someone or somewhere else, possibly the Leasowes. He also obtained 'the intire manadgement' of Curzon's grounds, perhaps leading to Emes leaving his post.

BELOW | Brown's competitors could be equally technically competent but seldom had his flair for design. At Dudmaston Hall, Shropshire, William Emes's plan shows he used similar features to Brown including a lake and shelter belts.

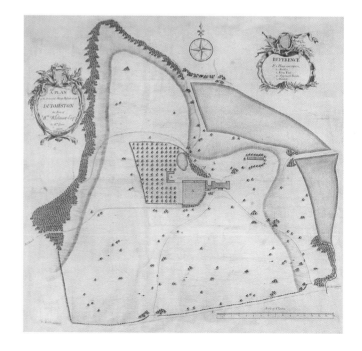

Emes set up independently as a landscape designer in 1760 at nearby Mackworth. His professional patch was centred on the north Midlands, Cheshire and Wales. His client list included many of the Tory gentry, unlike Brown who worked more often for Whig grandees. Emes was a proper 'improver' of estates as we see in his best works at Chirk and Erddig in Denbighshire, Hawkstone in Shropshire and Belton in Lincolnshire. Many commissions were in Staffordshire and in the counties around Derbyshire. At Etruria Hall (c.1768–71) for Josiah Wedgwood, who was greatly interested in gardening, he landscaped down to the canal and the Etruria Works, for which he was paid £117. Emes had various long-term jobs such as advising at Erddig, Chirk Castle and Sandon Hall over several decades, and at Margam Park, Keele Hall, Belton and Oakedge Park in Staffordshire.

Emes was renowned for water features, particularly long sinuous 'rivers'. He used canal-building techniques in his lakes, possibly picked up from canal engineers working in the area. These are seen in his methods of bank construction and in the Cylindrical Cascade at Erddig, a quick-drainage canal device. At Hawkstone he widened the River Hawk into a sublime, sinuous, river-like lake. It is a *tour de force*, of the quality of Brown, 1½ miles long, with a pronounced curve disguising one end. At Combermere the end of his curved lake wrapping around the pleasure grounds was further camouflaged in woodland.

In parks he used sunk fences or walls to break up paddocks into smaller, more manageable compartments, leaving the grazed parkland expanse looking seamless. He reintroduced flower gardens in some places, such as Sandon Hall, pre-empting Humphry Repton's style in the early nineteenth century. Like Brown he was a master of the unfolding view, his approach drives carefully revealing views by stages.

While he had moments of inspiration in his designs he did not equal Brown's relentless creativity. His plans for Keele and Oakedge appear less imaginative than Brown's for Ingestre (1756) and Trentham (1759). This was made up for by his competence, with sound professional advice and assistance. For the client he was reliable, reasonably priced and always in the area (unlike Brown who was all over the place and could be hard to pin down). He worked with architects, particularly Joseph Pickard of Derby, the Wyatts and John Soane. Later on he moved to Brockenhurst, Hampshire and did several jobs in the south, working with his former foreman John Webb (1754–1828), and died aged around 74. Webb went on to have a successful career himself as an architect and landscaper, working on more than 30 sites all over England.

Nathaniel Richmond (1723–84) was, like White, another escapee from Brown's home team, who built up a considerable portfolio and reputation, being called a 'Scholar of Browne'. He worked on his own account in the 1760s–80s and traversed the country, with between 30 and 40 commissions, possibly more, but seems to have been at heart a Home Counties man. He lived in Rickmansworth, Hertfordshire in the later 1750s, adjacent to Moor Park, where as foreman he oversaw Brown's design and for this was paid several thousands of pounds. He worked for Brown at nearby Chalfont Park and possibly at the Duke of Northumberland's Syon Park.

By 1759, after about six years with Brown, Richmond had set out on his own and acquired some renown in landscape gardening. He started a nursery in London's Marylebone at the edge of the fashionable West End with a practice as surveyor, improver and nurseryman. His first commission was for a knight with City interests, Sir Kenrick Clayton, at Marden Park, Surrey. He became renowned for laying out pleasure grounds, and his walled gardens and greenhouses were also notable. His Home Counties commissions spanned Hertfordshire, Bedfordshire, Buckinghamshire, Sussex and Surrey. Between 1759 and 1784 he worked on at least 30 sites. These included Harleyford, Buckinghamshire (for Sir Kenrick's brother, in the late 1760s), rather than Brown as has been thought, although it was in Brown's style and indicates that Richmond was greatly influenced by his previous master.

ABOVE | Emes laid out the grounds at Chirk Castle, Wrexham, and in 1767 designed a Neo-classical pavilion, the so-called `Retreat Seat' overlooking the concealed ha-ha.

Richmond was known to those in influential gardening circles including Charles Churchill of Chalfont Park, Buckinghamshire. One important commission was at nearby Shardeloes (1763–9) to transform the formal canal-and-avenue landscape, creating a long lake in the valley below the house perched on the hillside. Richmond was paid £1,000 and his foreman Henshaw £1,300 for this work. Richmond's reputation was well established by the 1770s when he advised at a group of Devon sites including Saltram. He visited nearby Killerton several times between 1777 and 1782, staying for a few days at a time, for which he was paid £20 per visit. He was probably most comfortable working within the Home Counties on villa landscapes, but even so he made competent forays into the design of the large landed estate. Like Brown he died relatively young, aged about 60.

Adam Mickle I, Brown's long-term foreman, finally set up on his own in 1779. Like White, he went north and was based at Bedale, North Yorkshire. His son was also Adam, who followed his father's career; some commissions may be by Adam II, and there was possibly an Adam III. Commissions connected with their name include Brancepeth Castle (1783), Tredegar

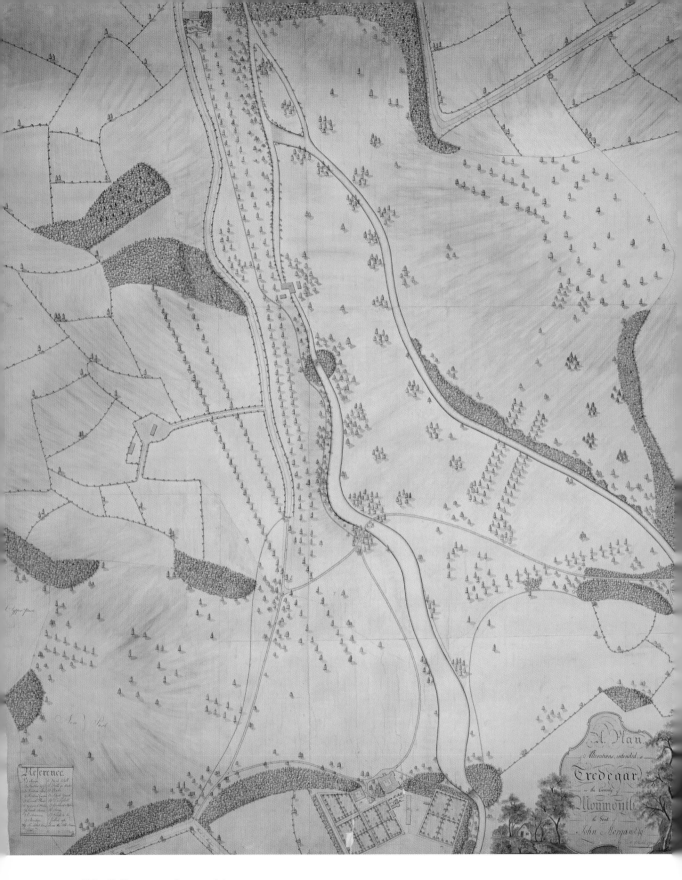

House (1788) and Piercefield (1790s) in south Wales, and Sutton Park and Swinton Castle, both in North Yorkshire, c.1790s. Adam II may have worked at Sandbeck and there is an Adam Mickle in Baines's *Directory* of 1823 as a landscape gardener.

Richard Woods (c.1716–93) was based in East Anglia, working on many Essex jobs and in the south of England. He was a Catholic surveyor and obtained commissions from some of the major Catholic families. As well as major schemes, he is known for working at a smaller scale, particularly on pleasure grounds and for his use of flowers. The first of his 45 known jobs was in 1758 at Buckland, Oxfordshire, laying out the park, supplying plants and designing various garden buildings. In 1759 Hartwell House, Buckinghamshire was landscaped, sweeping away the formal layout framed by tall clipped hedges recorded in a series of paintings in 1738. He landscaped the grounds of five houses by architect James Paine including Wardour Castle in Wiltshire for the Catholic Baron Arundell.

His rates for advice and supervision were fairly modest. At Hartwell he was paid 1 guinea a day when he worked there on the pleasure ground for Sir William Lee in 1759 and 1760. He was paid for 32 days of his time in ten visits of between one to five days, and 2 guineas for a design for a greenhouse and pinery (for that most sought-after of fruit, pineapples).

At Wardour Woods he was one of a succession of designers called in and sometimes called back, as happened quite often. Brown started there with a plan in 1754, followed by Joseph Spence who advised on improvements

OPPOSITE | Adam Mickle's 1788 extensive design for Tredegar, Newport, South Wales, was not entirely executed but the sinuous lake is a triumph.

BELOW | Richard Woods worked in south-east England. At Hartwell House, Buckinghamshire, he transformed a rigid French-style layout of hedged allees and a rectangular canal into a flowing park, lake and pleasure ground.

relating to Brown's plan, for which he charged £77, then Woods advised from 1764–72, being paid around £4,000, and then Brown was called back but his proposals were not carried out. In the end neither scheme was entirely realised, but Woods's Great Terrace, a spectacular mile-long walk along the foot of a steep woodland bank, was much admired along with its extensive views. It was planted with oak, silver fir, elm, beech, holly and laurel, under-planted with ornamental shrubs and flowers.

Like Brown, Woods employed several foremen to supervise works, as well as draughtsmen and surveyors. Like Brown's, Woods's drawings are not very polished. Latterly his career dwindled and from 1780 he had few and only small commissions, dying aged around 77.

BELOW | Robert Greening's 1750s plan of Wimpole pleasure ground in Cambridgeshire, drawn up before Brown worked on the park there in the 1760s.

The Greenings were a rather confusing gardening dynasty some of whom were Royal Gardeners. Their nursery business at Brentford was near the Thames, next to Syon Park and opposite royal Kew. This was a convenient place for enterprising and talented men to pick up design-and-build work. The dynasty began with Thomas (c.1684–1757) and continued with his sons, who were contemporaries of Brown. After 1738 Thomas the elder maintained the gardens Queen Caroline had laid out with William Kent at Richmond Gardens, now part of Kew Gardens. They had major contracts with the royal family and aristocracy. They were paid over £3,000 for work on the Duke of Cumberland's projects at Windsor (1747–8). Thomas the younger apparently provided designs at Kirtlington, Oxfordshire, where he was followed by Brown around 1752, the Gnoll near Windsor, and Corsham Court, Wiltshire where he was again followed by Brown. In 1751 he took on Kensington Gardens and St James's Palace, dying in 1757 a few months before his father. John Greening was head gardener and steward at Claremont for the Duke of Newcastle, working with William Kent and was Brown's predecessor at Hampton Court. Robert Greening worked in royal gardens including at Kew in the 1750s, and in c.1752 produced elaborate designs for a pleasure ground at Wimpole, Cambridgeshire. The family largely vanished

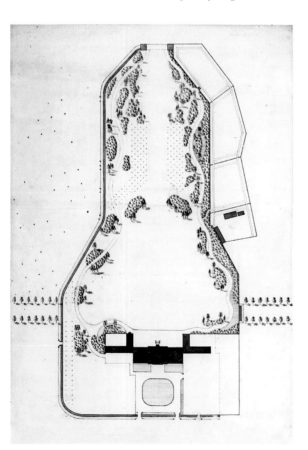

into obscurity as designers by the 1760s but not before a 'Mr Greening' was paid large sums for work at Windsor between 1762 and 1765.

Still more shadowy is **James Sanderson (1723–77)**, surveyor and nurseryman of Caversham, Oxfordshire, another Brown foreman, who left him in 1763. His connection with Brown is that he worked with his surveyor Donn in the 1760s. He laid out the park at Claydon House, Buckinghamshire, in the 1760s and 1770s, for which a plan survives.

Others of the numerous but often obscure landscapers working around the same time were Nathaniel Kent, Francis Richardson, William Speechley and Samuel Driver. Some went Continental. The Scots plantsman and gardener Thomas Blaikie was involved with some of the great Paris landscaping schemes in the 1770s and became a favourite of Marie Antoinette. Several men made it to Anglophile Russia. William Gould from Ormskirk laid out gardens for Prince Potemkin in St Petersburg, and a Scot, Charles Cameron, did the same at Pavlovsk. James Meader, having been gardener to the Duke of Northumberland at Syon, triumphantly laid out the grounds for Empress Catherine the Great at her English Palace at Peterhof. Meader was a disciple of Brown and published several books including *The Planter's Guide* (1779). Thomas Browne (1702–80) was a well-regarded land surveyor, and rather bizarrely a herald of arms, mapping estates mainly in Yorkshire and southern England. His own soubriquet was Sense Browne, to distinguish him from 'Capability'.

ABOVE | The Greenings worked on Windsor Great Park, Berkshire, from 1740 to the 1760s for the Ranger, the Duke of Cumberland, in the newly fashionable naturalistic style (after Thomas Sandby, 1772).

Architects – another breed

Brown on his country-estate commissions worked alongside the great architects of the day: Robert Adam, James Paine, William Chambers, James Wyatt and plenty of others. He also worked alongside local builders, including the Hiorns brothers in the Midlands. He did not employ architects directly as this was left to the client.

The mastery of Adam and Chambers was officially recognised by the time Brown got to his royal position at Hampton Court in 1764, where they were both installed as the two chief Architects of the Office of Works. Brown's architectural skill stands up well against them. His Lion Bridge at Burghley is of the same quality as similar bridges by Paine (Lion Bridge at Alnwick, the road bridge at Wallington, and at Chatsworth), Chambers (New Bridge, Blenheim) and Adam (the road bridge at Audley End). Sometimes it is a mystery who designed some bridges, whether Brown or another architect employed at the same time, as for the drive bridge at Compton Verney, which could be by Adam or Brown.

ABOVE | Robert Adam was one of the finest Georgian architects who designed buildings for many parks, including those by Brown. His bridge at Kedleston, Derbyshire, is one of his many garden buildings there, together with the house.

While Adam was charming and easy to work with Chambers was not, and he had a high opinion of his own worth. In designing the royal grounds at Kew for Princess Augusta, George III's widowed mother, Chambers put up nearly two dozen garden buildings, many large, such as the Orangery. His scheme was crowned by the monumental ten-storey Chinese Pagoda, brightly coloured, and complete with dozens of gold dragons glaring down from the roofs (he had visited China on business in the 1740s). This assortment of buildings populated a rather fragmented and complicated layout alongside Brown's sweeping riverside groves and lawns for the King. After his mother's death in 1772, the King united both in one vast garden and cancelled a planned new palace designed by Chambers, much to the latter's chagrin. The architect then stuck firmly to designing buildings, at which he was very successful, and largely withdrew from garden design.

The prickly and self-promoting Chambers was a mass communicator, unlike Brown. He also harboured a grudge, and set himself up to rival and criticise Brown. Like Adams and others he published books of his architectural designs, always a good marketing move. In his 'Dissertation' on garden design in 1772 he also took pot shots at Brown's style, criticising its natural effect against his favoured formality. Walpole noted that it was written in 'wild revenge against Brown' and Chambers took considerable flak for daring to cast aspersions about the by-now revered Brown. Walpole reckoned that the only surprising consequence was that 'it is laughed at, and is not likely to be adopted'. Poor Chambers must have fizzed with rage. He clearly did not have much of a sense of humour about himself. Brown, he implied, was one of the ranks of those 'peasants' who 'emerge from the melon grounds to commence professors', for he and his like were merely kitchen gardeners, 'well skilled in the culture of salads, but little acquainted with the principles of ornamental gardening'. However, the overwhelming aristocratic patronage of Brown's skills refuted Chambers's vitriol. Brown did not retaliate, but merely carried on regardless, laughing all the way to the bank.

BELOW | William Chambers, another great Georgian architect, designed many garden buildings, some in Brown's landscapes, as well as Princess Augusta's gardens at the Royal Botanic Gardens Kew (Valentine Green, 1780).

Brown's Professional Legacy

Brown's work was so extensive and impressive that inevitably it left the most influential legacy of all English landscape designers. This bequest to the world was huge, but naturally his style was amended as fashions changed.

Five years after Brown's death Humphry Repton took up the baton. His ambition was to become the nation's most well-known and prolific landscape designer to the wealthy and aspiring, just like Brown, beginning in 1788 and continuing until just before his death in 1818. He was a fan of Brown, proclaiming so in print, and was given all his office plans by son Lance (sadly now vanished).

After Brown died came Romanticism: mountains, wilderness and the frisson of danger and fear were favoured and sought out by persons of taste and tourists. Repton went to war, if only in print, championing Brown and his perceived smoother style, with two bad-tempered and otherwise largely obscure members of the landed gentry, Uvedale Price and Richard Payne-Knight. Coming from the craggy Welsh borders they considered themselves arbiters of the more rugged Picturesque taste. They enthusiastically engaged Repton in the Picturesque Controversy, an overblown spat that didn't really have much effect. The Picturesque was not so different to Brown's own style. It was just a more rugged offshoot of the English Landscape Park. Price and Knight unfairly caricatured Brown's style as too smoothly formulaic, turning its back on the wider landscape setting, and lacking the frisson of the scarily jagged and sublime that they promoted. This was belied most clearly by Brown's last great park, Berrington, in which he warmly embraced the wider Herefordshire landscape, but even so it was not exactly scary. Try the vast Picturesque Hafod in mid-Wales for that emotion.

Throughout the Industrial Revolution Brown's style continued to be admired and emulated by wealthy new park makers. Waddesdon Manor was a very late flowering of Brown's country-estate style at a huge scale in the 1880s. It was the setting for Ferdinand de Rothschild's huge Frenchified mansion in Buckinghamshire, designed by a Frenchman, Elie Lainé.

The formula was so flexible that it even influenced the many new public parks that sprang up in towns and cities worldwide for the workers of the Industrial Revolution, who appreciated water, grass and trees in the Brownian style as much as their wealthy masters. Beginning with Loudon's

Derby Arboretum and Paxton's Birkenhead Park in the 1840s, the public park movement snowballed, the child of the Omnipotent Magician Brown and the English Landscape Park.

Across the Continent the English Landscape Garden was interpreted as the Jardin Anglais and Englische Garten. It was taken up enthusiastically as far away as Sweden via F. M. Piper, and in Russia by Catherine the Great. Over the Pond probably the greatest exponent was the American politician and polymath Thomas Jefferson who became a sympathetic interpreter after his European tour of 1785–86. Among a packed itinerary he saw Brown's Claremont, Caversham, Wotton, Stowe, Blenheim and Moor Park, and was deeply influenced by their artistry as settings for buildings. His home, Monticello in Virginia, is breathtaking. Standing on top of a hill, it has wonderful panoramic views across the hills and valleys around. In turn Jefferson greatly influenced the American greats of landscape design, Andrew Jackson Downing and Frederick Law Olmsted, and so his style spread across North America.

BELOW | Brown's influence spread worldwide. US President Thomas Jefferson saw the greatest parks in England and was inspired by them in his North American estate Monticello, Virginia.

Sites to visit

All the following have a significant Brown layer unless otherwise noted. Please see individual websites for visitor information and opening hours.

1. Alnwick Castle and Hulne Park, Northumberland
2. Ampthill Park, Bedfordshire
3. Ashridge, Hertfordshire (NT)
4. Audley End, Essex
5. Basildon Park, Berkshire (NT)
6. Berrington Hall, Herefordshire (NT)
7. Blenheim Palace, Oxfordshire
8. Bowood House and Gardens, Wiltshire
9. Burton Constable, East Yorkshire
10. Charlecote, Warwickshire (NT)
11. Chatsworth, Derbyshire
12. Clandon Park, Surrey (NT)
13. Claremont Landscape Garden, Surrey (NT)
14. Compton Verney, Warwickshire
15. Coombe Abbey, Warwickshire
16. Croome Court, Worcestershire (NT)
17. Erddig, Wrexham (William Emes) (NT)
18. Gatton Park, Surrey (NT)
19. Gibside, Tyne and Wear (NT)
20. Harewood House, West Yorkshire
21. Hatfield Forest, Essex (NT)
22. Highclere, Hampshire
23. Ickworth, Suffolk (NT)
24. Kedleston Hall, Derbyshire (Robert Adam and William Emes) (NT)
25. Killerton, Devon (Nathaniel Richmond) (NT)
26. Kirkharle, Northumberland
27. Lacock Abbey, Wiltshire (NT)
28. Langley Park, Buckinghamshire
29. Longleat, Wiltshire
30. Luton Hoo, Bedfordshire
31. Milton Abbey, Dorset
32. Moccas Park, Herefordshire
33. Newton House (Dinefwr Castle), Carmarthenshire (NT)
34. Petworth, West Sussex (NT)
35. Prior Park, Somerset (NT)

36. Rothley Lakes (Wallington Estate), Northumberland (NT)
37. Royal Botanic Gardens, Kew, Surrey (Brown and William Chambers)
38. Saltram, Devon (Nathaniel Richmond) (NT)
39. Sheffield Park, East Sussex (NT)
40. Stourhead, Wiltshire (Henry Hoare) (NT)
41. Stowe, Buckinghamshire (NT)
42. Syon Park, Greater London
43. Temple Newsam, West Yorkshire
44. Tredegar, Newport, South Wales (Adam Mickle) (NT)
45. Trentham Gardens, Staffordshire
46. Uppark, West Sussex (NT)

47. Wallington, Northumberland (NT)
48. Warwick Castle, Warwickshire
49. Weston Park, Staffordshire
50. Wimpole, Cambridgeshire (NT)
51. Woodchester, Gloucestershire (NT)
52. Wotton Underwood, Buckinghamshire
53. Wrest Park, Bedfordshire

Further reading

The guide books to those sites that open to the public provide information about specific places that Brown worked on. Other works on Brown and his times:

Bapasola, Jeri, *The Finest View in England. The Landscape and Gardens at Blenheim Palace* (Blenheim Palace, 2009)

Brown, Jane, *Lancelot 'Capability' Brown: The Omnipotent Magician* (Pimlico, 2012)

Laird, Mark, *The Flowering of the Landscape Garden* (Penn, 1999)

Dictionary of National Biography (Oxford, online at www.oxforddnb.com)

Mowl, Timothy, *Gentlemen and Players: Gardeners of the English Landscape* (Sutton, 2000)

Phillips, Charlotte and Shane, Nora, *John Stuart 3rd Earl of Bute 1713–92* (Luton Hoo Estate, 2014)

Shrimpton, Colin, *A History of Alnwick Parks and Pleasure Grounds* (Northumberland Estates, 2006)

Stroud, Dorothy, *'Capability' Brown* (Faber & Faber, 3rd edn, 1975)

Williamson, Tom, *Polite Landscapes: Gardens and Society in Eighteenth-century England* (Tempus, 1995)

Picture Credits

Index

Page numbers in *italic* refer to illustrations

Acknowledgements

I would particularly like to thank the following people for their generosity in sharing their information and thoughts, although any errors are of course entirely my own.

From the National Trust I would like to thank David Adshead (Head Curator); Katherine Alker (Head Gardener, Croome); Katie Bond (National Trust Publisher); Mike Calnan (Head of Gardens); Roger Carr-Whitworth (Curator); Chris Connell (Volunteer Researcher, Hatfield Forest); Simon Cranmer (General Manager, Hatfield Forest); Stephanie Evans (Curator) re Newtown and Tredegar; Amy Feldman (Editor: General Books and Guidebooks); Kevin Henry (Newton House); Paul Hewett (Countryside Manager, Wallington); Oonagh Kennedy (Curator); Mark Lamey (Gardens Adviser and 'Capability' Brown 300 Co-ordinator); Lloyd Langley (House and Collections Manager, Wallington); James Rothwell (Curator) re Ickworth; Martin Sadler (Petworth); Lisa Voden-Decker (Curator) re Wimpole; Richard Wheeler (National Specialist Historic Landscapes).

I would also like to thank Mr and Mrs J Anderson (Kirkharle); Clare Baxter (Collections and Archive Manager, Northumberland Estates, Alnwick Castle); Sarah Couch (re Gatton); Susan Darling (London Parks and Gardens Trust researcher, re Syon); Ceryl Evans (Director, CB300 Festival); Nigel Ferrier (owner, Fenstanton Manor House); Chris Gallagher (re Berrington, Charlecote and historic trees); David Gladstone (owner, Wotton Underwood); Michael Harrison (Garden Manager, Wotton Underwood); Virginia Hinze (re Ashburnham); Christopher Hunwick (Archivist, Northumberland Estates, Alnwick Castle); Rosemary Jury (Buckinghamshire Gardens Trust); Jonathan Lovie (The Garden History Society); Janette Ray (Garden Historian); Kristy Richardson (Senior Editor, Pavilion); Fran Sands (Soane Museum, re Adam); Chris Sumner (re Kew); Peter Taylor (Commissioning Editor, Pavilion); Mick Thompson (Archivist, Ashridge Business School); Jenifer White (National Landscape Adviser, Historic England); Nigel Wilkins (Historic England Archive).